MW00411731

CHOOSE

DIFFERENT

Keith McCoy

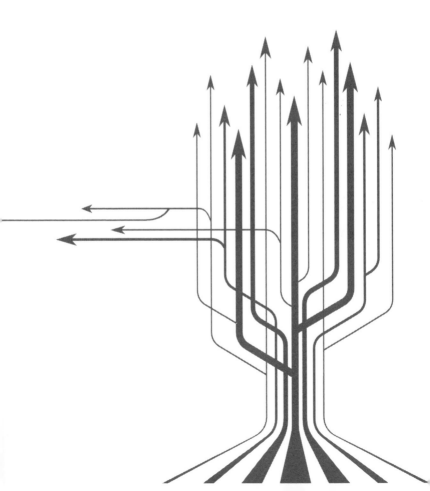

CHOOSE

DIFFERENT

for

Riley
Reagan
Ryder
Render
Remedy
River
Rhys
and
R........

and Keri.
none of this happens
without you

FOREWARD

Riley Reign is the owner and curator of the *Spirit and Soul Blog*, an educator on Inspired Transformation and a writer, published in online journals such as *Thrive*, *The Elephant Journal* and *Yogi Approved*. She is uniquely suited to speak on choices and the ideals presented here because she is also my oldest child and has been present for much of the discovery described within.

The person that wrote this book and the person I grew up with as a child are two very different people. However, both of them are my father, and my lifelong teachers. I am equally grateful for both of them, because they have both taught me many lessons in life, both together and separately. Of course, I could say that I love one version of them more, but without the man my dad was 10 years ago we wouldn't have the man he is now. Because without discomfort and negative experiences we would not know how to grow, rise, or Choose Different.

Perhaps it is insane to say, but I am incredibly blessed from the discomfort my dad had to grow through, which influenced some discomfort and growing of my own, because it taught me how to be able to grow, rise, and to Choose Different, too. While that doesn't mean that it was, or is, ever easy, the perspective, hindsight, and insight can make it easier to practice the principles held within this book. It takes courage to say that you want more for yourself and in this world. I can't say why or how that happened for my dad, but what I do know is that harnessing the courage to Choose Different is one of the most impactful and meaningful things you can do to shift your reality.

When we live in our passion, our growth, and our mission, we can inspire others to begin living in theirs, too. I can say as a lifelong observer and personal witness, that Keith McCoy has claimed that courage again and again as his growth has asked him to, resistant or not, and he continuously chooses to live in his passion, through growth, and on mission. Is it sometimes scary as hell? Yes. Will you have to grow and rise through the discomfort of your new choices? Yes. And, the world will be better off for it. You get to decide whether or not it is worth it, and Choose Different will surely help you make that decision for yourself.

When you think of someone that is larger than life in life, business, and most importantly presence, what kind of person do you think of? Someone that shows up more than they could ever be expected or predicted to? Someone that is beyond giving of themselves? Someone that is not only determined, but fiercely dedicated to their work and their *Why* (i.e. the Tony Robbins', Gary Vee's, and Oprah's of today's world)? Ideally, is this also someone that you desire to become?

I've decided to call these people giants. Some of them are gentle but don't seem so at first glance. Some of them are loud and have lots to say, and many of them are emperors and empresses. Some of them are not-so-secret giants. I'm sure we all know a few of those. The author of this book in your hands, and my rad father, Keith McCoy, is one of them and as his oldest daughter (a.k.a the one that has seen the most of his transformation) I can say that all of my siblings will likely grow to be giants of their own, because we've had such a powerful and willing example in my father.

I personally have been able to create and cultivate my own career and platform because of the example my parents lead by. Each and every one of us has the opportunity and capability to Choose Different, often in life altering ways. I know that this may be an intense statement to read, and I'd like to invite you to see it instead with it's empowering truth. I get to live my life authentically, full of passion, growth, and mission, because my parents have paved the way. They continue to do that for everyone they can serve, and my father expands upon that in a very powerful way with this book.

Choose Different asks the question, "Are you living your life by default or by design?" and unlike other books that propose similar questions, this one gives you a cheat code, a every simple and powerful way to create change for yourself if you wish to. If you aren't living your life by design and really want to but aren't sure how, you will find your answer in Choose Different. If you are living your life by design, and want to elevate that design to something next-level, Choose Different will remind you just how you get to choose what your life looks like and it will bring inspiration and clarity to how you can begin to elevate the imprint you are designing.

I am sure that you are reading this book because of some kind of calling, subconscious or otherwise, to lead a legacy. Whatever that legacy may be, whatever it sounds like, looks like, or wants to become, I want you to know that if you read this book with an open and willing heart, mind, and soul, and you implement the very simple yet sometimes uncomfortable tool of choosing different, you will begin cultivating, expanding, and living your legacy.

I have complete confidence that Choose Different has the capacity to serve every single person that reads it. It is up to you to allow this book and it's teachings to influence you. I have complete confidence that Choose Different will meet any curious creator exactly where they are at within their journey, and can provide meaningful building blocks that can be used for any creation.

Keith writes a genuine exploration and life changing teaching of what it means to Choose Different, accrediting his own personal journey, experiences, and exploration along the way. Not only is Choose Different a tool crafted of universal truth, it is the blueprint for beginning (or continuing) to both claim and change your life, your story, and experience.

This is a story about how all of us are broken to some degree, and how that likely hard to face fact doesn't even matter. This is a story of how we choose our own destiny, and how we get to choose to be empowered. This book is not merely an expression of coming from nothing and creating success and happiness for oneself, or coming from something terrible and being able to grow through it. This book is an expression of how it doesn't really matter where you come from, where you've been, or even where you are, because you get to choose what happens next.

I hope you are ready to unlock your own life, Choose Different for the benefit of yourself and those around you, and to never go back. Because this is your story. It doesn't matter where you come from, where or who you've been, or even where you are. You get to choose who you are now. You get to Choose Different. You get to choose what happens next.

INTRODUCTION

I will never know all of the answers...although I never wanna know anyway

Manifesto II, Nahko & Medicine for the People

I have been doing this thing called life for over 40 years now. In that time the growth I have experienced has been tremendous. I have had mentors and coaches who have guided me and helped me to muddle through the fog. They have loved me and served me as a person without expecting anything in return. Along this path, one that I truly hope is far from over, I have been exposed to a variety of tools that have helped me navigate life with joy and understanding. Some of these tools I believe saved my marriage, others my relationship with my children and others still, my life. Along the way I have discovered that some of the concepts I have been introduced to and adopted are universally true. Please consider that the preceding statement is coming from a person who really doesn't like to operate in absolutes. Reflecting back on every thing I have learned, I would still argue that there is so much left to be learned. It is often attributed to Socrates to have said "The man who is truly wise knows that he knows very little" and I have also come to believe this to be true. There is much I have learned, and yet I am constantly working to remain open to the idea that those ideals and tools already learned are fluid, and as we learn and grow the nuances of life are expandable, and often times can use some fine tuning.

Coming to some of these realizations has sometimes felt like a kick in the teeth. Occasionally it has brought things into perfect alignment and made complete sense, reminiscent of those 'aha moments' you've possibly heard Oprah talk about. Or maybe you haven't. What is important to note here is that most of these realizations I resisted for years. Then, when I finally accepted them to be true, I resisted still, often due to my own pride; who wants to be left thinking "Now I have to admit that I was wrong"? What I wasn't prepared to face then, and have now since realized, is that more often not, I am usually the least at peace when I am not open to exploration. I have found that if you take the time to sit with your thoughts, to understand where they are coming from, and to ask yourself some key questions, without the emotionally connected and oft confused story behind it, you may very well be able to move forward. In fact, I am certain of it. All it requires, and perhaps the most difficult of tasks, is the releasing of your ego.

To help underline the journey I've experienced I'd like to share a bit of my early years with you, if I may. I believe it may help you to understand a little where I am coming from and how the ideas presented later came to be. I was born into the textbook definition of a dysfunctional family. My father was a police officer and an Air Force Veteran, having served in the Vietnam War. As I've been told, my mother was a convenience store clerk at the time of my birth. Dad was one in a long line of military men, and his upbringing was filled with uncertainty from early on with an abundance of traveling and an assuredly unhealthy environment of physical and emotional abuse. Dad was the oldest of 8 and living quarters were tight. His father, my grandfather, was a stern man and from what I can gather they were a cared for family but not a happy one.

My mother was the youngest of three and born in Georgia to a very traditional southern family. By all accounts she was supposed to have been born a boy, and so her father decided that their youngest would be named Jimmie. Well, lo and behold *she* was not a *he*, but the name was decided on and so Jimmie Nell it was. Her mother, my maternal grandmother, was also a stern one and very southern indeed. When Jimmie's parents split Grandmother took all her children and moved up north to Chicago. Somewhere along the way Jimmie Nell found her way to Las Vegas where she met, married my father, and had me.

If the stories I've been told are true, both of my parents drank heavily and often and partook in recreational drug use. It was the 1970's. Their marriage was passionate, violent and loud if anything. Not surprisingly they were divorced when I was about 2 1/2. With that, Mom and I moved from Las Vegas back to Chicago, Cicero to be exact, to be closer to her family. Cicero in the 1970's was, and largely still is, known for its gang violence and high crime rate. So it was still a loud and chaotic environment. Tragically, within a year of moving to Cicero my mother was shot and killed. The specifics of that evening are muddled and lost in time for now. The best I have been able to gather is that she was involved with a man whom she would have been better off without and that it is quite possible he had her killed. The loss of my mother was a circumstance that would shape the next 20 plus years of my life.

My father had remarried by the time my mother was killed and they were expecting a child of their own. So upon my mothers death I went to live with my father and his new family at the age of 3 1/2. My new step-mother (who I often refer to simply as my mother, so I apologize for the confusion this may bring down the road) brought a daughter from a previous marriage into the fold and my father had yet another daughter from a marriage that had failed before the one to my own biological mother.....confused yet? Needless to say we had a full house and a blended family before blended family was the politically correct term for it.

My oldest sister at the time was living with her biological mother and so she was not particularly in the picture. I'm not sure when I actually met my oldest sister to be honest, but I do know it was years after this. At about the age of 5, if I recall correctly, I was told that my mother had committed suicide. I know now that it was pretty widely accepted that this official word was not true but for reasons beyond my understanding my parents felt it best to tow that line then. As one could imagine, this obviously effected me in deep ways, both consciously and subconsciously. To this day I struggle with the realities of suicide in a sometimes irrational way.

My maternal grandparents, assumably in their despair from losing their youngest daughter, fought very hard to gain custody of me. In only what I can assume was a longing for a stable connection to their daughter it seemed they felt it was their duty to raise me. Knowing what they knew, or thought they knew, about my father's less than ideal lifestyle, and seemingly unwilling to accept that of their own daughters, it seems as though they were desperate to stay connected to my mother in some way. This became over time an ugly legal battle with numerous appearances in court and it did not go well for them in the end. Upon the ruling of the court they were barred from seeing me at all until I was of legal age. To this day I am not clear on what's exactly true and what's fiction. Each of the players have their own version of the story, each just similar enough to be reasonable, and yet each varied enough to lead to confusion. My own recollection of the proceedings is muddy at best, if not nonexistent. I recall being called into the judges chambers at one point and being asked point blank white whom I wanted to live with. At age 6 I do not think I was at all capable of making a clear and sound decision at all. I chose to live with my father and new baby sister. In reality, none of the details are relevant or matters anymore. The decision had been made, the impact of which were already rippling. and I now had a permanent address.

It turned out to be a violent and angry address. Both physically and emotionally tumultuous and by today's standards certainly abusive. Enough so that from the age of 12-16 I lived in a children's home as a way to get me away from the situation, and to give my parents a reprieve as well. Both parties were tasked with learning how to get along with one another and to face their demons with enough space to do so in relative peace. When I returned home at age 16, anticipating a new Rockwellian life, my parents decided to separate. It seemed evident to me at that time, that while I spent the last 4 years in counseling, breaking old habits and learning new ones, their work had been left quite undone. So while I was back living at home, this was not a home I, nor many others within it, wanted to be a part of. It was a home filled with resentment, anger, miscommunication and illness, both physical and mental, all coupled with a lack of money or the appropriate tools to address any of it.

It stayed that way until I left directly after graduating high school and just before my 18th birthday. I was so desperate to leave that I slept on a couch belonging to one of my only friends for months. I owned a car, but no driver's license (my parents refused to sign off on that due to my 'behavior' and the cost of insurance), a backpack of clothes and some odds and ends. So here I was, an adult, on my own, and everything I had learned in therapy was no longer relevant or being applied. I am not even sure that I learned anything throughout that experience other than how to manipulate a conversation. If I had it was all but replaced with bitterness, anger and a resounding victim mentality. In this space and time I was quite certain I had wasted my time if I had in fact learned anything of importance.

While my parents may have failed at parenting in most people's eyes, they were also wildly aware of this. In the years since have spent countless hours discussing the upbringing I had, all of our roles in it, and many years healing wounds and relationships. My relationship with my father is sound and healthy today. We understand one another, we speak regularly and I respect him now more than I did as a young adult. We understand boundaries and we love each other. Unfortunately my step mother passed before we had a chance to completely resolve our issues. I'd like to say I did everything I could have done to heal that relationship, but I am afraid that would be a lie. There was more that I could have done. And like everything, I will live with the results of my choices. I have come to terms with the fact that there are unresolved circumstances surrounding the finality of our relationship.

I share this brief history with you because based on traditional socio-economic patterns and behaviors, the person described to you above should not be in the position I am currently in today. Based on traditional trajectories when I left high school, and the community I grew up in, I should have been in a gang, doing drugs, beating women, and all manners of behaviors associated with poor anger management skill fueled by recreational use of drugs and alcohol. The reality is that while I did my fair share of some of those things I was able to remain drug free and out of prison. I've spent a night or two in jail and until about the age of 30 I was on a pretty dark path for sure. I found it hard to respect authority, found it nearly impossible to truly love others and was quick to sabotage a relationship whether it was a casual or intimate one, including, sadly, those relationships with my wife and children.

And I was angry. More than anything there was so much anger. Couple that with my rich Irish Heritage (yes, I am a descendant of the Hatfield/McCoy McCoy's) and that anger was violent. In case you weren't aware, anger and violence are destructive. My life was destructive if it was anything. If you had asked me during that time why things were the way they were, why my relationships had failed or were failing, why my career was a stagnant mess of one job after another, or why my financial situation was always on the brink of collapse, I would gladly share with you my sad, sad story in hopes you would understand how life had just dealt me a bad hand. In my mind I was a victim, and you were suppose to just forgive my madness because it wasn't my fault. It was my parent's fault. It was my boss's fault. It was my wife, my daughters, or my in law's fault. It was life's fault. It was rarely my fault.

The truth is it wasn't any of 'their' fault. My folks did the best they could with what they had. And the sad reality for them, and in return for me, was that they had little to nothing to work with. For any tradesmen to be successful you have to have tools. Parents are not any different. My birth mother was killed in December 1977 and my Dad's new wife was 7 months pregnant. While she thought she was having one kid, she got two. Add that to the one she had already, and his other daughter from a previous marriage and, well, WOW, here was a nice size little nuclear family. Four kids, none of whom had the same two parents, to be raised by this couple who were so poorly equipped that in all actuality they weren't prepared to raise one, let alone all of them.

I share all of this with you not to disparage anyone, least of all my parents. They did their dead level best with an empty tool box. And quite frankly, all things being equal, they did a pretty good job with what they had. I have no ill will or judgement toward any of them. I deeply love and appreciate all they have done for me. My intention with this book is to bring to light for you what I believe to be one of the most important, if not the most important, principles that defines how I move about my days, weeks and life now. It is to share with you how I was able to come from the life described above and live this - I have been married to the same amazing woman for 20 years. We have 7 (soon to be 8) beautiful kids together. Even though I tried my damnedest in the beginning to sabotage this relationship, and I certainly caused her some pain, she stuck by me. If not for her I do not know where I would be today. I will always maintain that she was the first to teach me that I deserved to be loved unconditionally. She taught me that I needed to love myself. Because of that I learned somewhere along the line that I had to take responsibility for me; for who I was and for the consequences of my actions.

I was forced to see the ripple effect my actions would cause and to hold myself accountable to those ripples. The reality is that in every single thing we do, consciously or otherwise, we leave a mark, there is a cause and an effect. In everything we do, we have a choice. We may often *feel* like we don't. And as we will discuss again, feelings aren't facts. I recently heard a quote that aligns perfectly with this concept - Reality is often harsh, but always fair. So when you step back and look at the reality of your life, if you truly want clarity, you must remove the emotion and see the situation for what it is: The result of your choices. Each choice has a ripple, a butterfly effect, that either affects us, and those around us, in a detrimental way or in a way that benefits us. We cannot get away from this universal truth. And the sooner you can realize, understand and truly appreciate that you are in control of your decisions, and that ultimately the choices you make are the most important thing in how you live your life, the sooner you can begin to live your life by design.

What
do
YOU
want?

chapter one
CONFUSION IS THE ENEMY

You will not be punished for your anger
You will be punished by your anger

Buddha

Confusion is the lack of clarity, or in other terms, the lack of understanding, and understanding brings clarity. When the question is posed "What do you want?" are you met with clarity or confusion? My bet is that there were multiple responses that flashed into your mind. Some serious, some comical and some may have caused you to think "where did that come from?" This is what we call confusion.

Of all the mental states we experience I believe confusion can be the most difficult to navigate. I think too few of us actually recognize confusion for what it actually is - and I would argue that it is either the root cause of all negative emotions, or an emotion in itself. It is quite possible that many people would not consider confusion an emotion, but I do.

Certainly we can agree though, that a state of confusion brings about one or all of the following emotional states -

- Boredom
- Pessimism/Frustration/Irritation/Impatience
- Overwhelm/Blame/Discouragement
- Anger
- Revenge

- Hatred/Rage
- Jealousy

Therefore, confusion could in fact be an emotional state in and of itself, considering we define emotion as a natural instinctive state of mind deriving from one's circumstances, mood, or relationships with others. However, I don't get to rewrite the emotional dictionary here (we will tap more into about what we can and cannot control in a later chapter) so for the purpose of this conversation we will just refer to confusion as a mental state.

Of all the emotions that are mentioned above I think it would be safe to say that the one that manifests the most, or is the most perceivable, in our day to day activities is anger. Boredom can lead to anger. Frustration or impatience often also show up as anger. So while many have said that anger is the enemy, I believe the true enemy is confusion. It is important to distinguish between the two because it is important to get to the root cause of our emotional conditions when determining how to choose different. Anger is the byproduct of confusion. It is a byproduct of when we tend to focus on what is happening to us and not for us. When we choose to mostly see the circumstances in our life that aren't going our way rather than finding gratitude for the things that are. When we are focused too much inward, and not enough outward, that is when confusion, and therefore anger, will rear it's ugly head.

The root of confusion is typically a cocktail of unmet expectations muddled with just the right amount of assumption. To be fair, ultimately what is an unmet expectation often, but not always, is simply your assumption. How often do you actually verbalize or somehow otherwise clearly communicate your expectations to others? If you do not, as most of us do not because we are either incapable or unwilling to, then you are assuming they know what you expect. And when the expectation isn't fully met you are left feeling let down, or angry. You're angry not because of what the offending party did, but what they failed to do, which was failing to meet your presumably un-communicated expectation. So unless they are psychic or have the ability to read between the lines at an expert level, they are doomed to fail and inevitably let you down. Therefore you must be destined to be angry, as this is the result of your choices. We can apply this scenario to almost every area in our lives. An unmet expectation is either rooted in, or leads us to assumption. Add to this that we compound the issue by often taking these things personally, as our mindset in this scenario is too inward. We are thinking it is about us. In reality our anger stems from the confusion that is the true end result.

The first thing to do in avoiding or preventing this apparent eventuality is to execute a new thought pattern. This requires the removal of the emotionally driven part of the story from the equation. What I mean by that is we must always be facing reality, or the facts. As outlined above, when we begin to feel within a situation or toward someone that we are angry it is often because of a failed understanding on our part with regard to what is actually happening. For example, your friend Joe doesn't meet your expectation, whatever that is, whether communicated to them or not. You are angry because they failed to do A, B or C. And in your mind they don't do A, B or C within a myriad of possible scenarios. Either you aren't good enough, or they had better things to do, and then it quickly spirals somehow into how they never show up for you and they've never loved you. Before we even know what has happened we create these self indulgent stories of how the world and everyone in it is treating us unfairly.

We have all had a friend that has not shown up after offering to or agreeing to help you with something. At first you react rationally, thinking to yourself 'They should be here in a few minutes'. As time goes by, you more than likely become angry or hurt - 'They said they would be here by 10. She is always letting me down'. And eventually when they don't show up at all your thoughts lead to something like 'I just can't count on her anymore' and then perhaps your thoughts eventually become 'Maybe something horrible happened, I hope she is OK'.

It is more typical that our thoughts begin within our own universe and how it impacts us personally, and then leads (hopefully) to compassion and concern for our friend. Yet those are typically the last thoughts in this scenario; while our primary thoughts are about ourselves and our needs. It's this monkey mind negative talk that we all have, rooted in our own view of self, our own self worth and our self imposed confusion that gets fueled by assumption and taking things personally. What if you could let go of that negative talk for what truly is happening; the person who said they could be there to help isn't. That's it. It has nothing to do with you, and everything to do with them. Perhaps when they agreed to help you they actually said, 'if they could' and you translated that into "I'll be there". Or maybe they did in fact agree to be there. Here we are, they didn't show up. It means nothing except that they aren't there. It means absolutely nothing about you, until they tell you that it does. And until then you can choose to just move forward, without judgement, without assumption and without confusion, and in peace. Because you choose to be at peace.

Obviously this is just one scenario set forth as an example. There are hundreds of additional scenarios and thousands of reasons that they could be true. And that is just it. Regardless of the size of, or the source of your confusion, it is as simple as claiming your own massively creative power and choosing how to respond to these thoughts that is within your control. It sounds ridiculously simple but it really comes down to that. Choosing peace. Take a moment and think of the most negatively impactful thoughts you have throughout your day and week, or month. Write them down and keep a record if you need to. In fact, I highly recommend it. I can almost guarantee you that you never consciously decided to think those thoughts. So where did they come from? Why are they there, and more importantly, what should we do with them?

The simplest solution is usually the best. And in this scenario, and nearly all others, that is also true. You simply get to choose what thoughts to hang onto and what thoughts to let go of. Which ones to believe, and which ones to see as false. And certainly false thoughts, or lies, are the ones you will want to let go of. It is confusion that arises when we aren't able to discern the lies from the reality. This confusion is quite possibly the root cause of our suffering. Notice that I didn't say earlier the simplest solution was the easiest. Discerning fact from fiction can be very challenging. When woking with matters of human nature this typically means we have to accept that as humans we like to hang on to the emotion of it, to hang on to the labels and to the story that supports our feelings.

The trouble is, Feelings are not Facts.

I invite you, when you are ready, to dive deep into this concept of meeting your thoughts with understanding, of learning how to discern feelings from facts, and of learning how to be a lover of reality. The best advice I can offer in terms of how to do that, is to get your hands on the work of Byron Katie. Her book, *Loving What Is,* and the tools she provides in it have changed my life. If you are open to it, and apply the tools she provides, I am confident it will change yours as well. Some of what I have shared here is my attempt to paint the broadest of pictures of what she delves into much more deeply and with much greater understanding.

Another path to take along this vein would be to dig deeper into Stoic philosophy. Much of what Byron Katie writes about fits into this philosophy. The writings of Epictetus, Seneca and Marcus Aurelius are the root of Stoicism and ideal places to start. If you prefer to see how ancient Roman philosophy relates to today's world directly, without having to make the correlation yourself, then get modern and dive into the work of Ryan Holiday's books *The Obstacle is the Way* or *The Daily Stoic.* The Cliff's Notes version is this: control what you can control and let go of the rest. Also described quite simply in the Latin phrase *Amor Fati,* or *to* "love one's fate." This sums up the attitude and the ideology of the Stoic in the simplest of terms. To love what is and to control the controllables. As you dissect these ideals further you should begin to get clarity as to what you can control and what you can't. Eventually it becomes clear that what we can control is how we show up, and virtually nothing else. How we feel about the external things in our world and how we look at the things that cause us to feel one way or another in the first place are ours to determine.

To this point, when we choose anger, most of us do not respond to that feeling well. It brings about rash judgement, lashing out at others over simple things., causes us to say things we do not mean, and can lead to other detrimental behaviors like drinking and poor eating habits. Anger often reduces our ability to make much needed sound judgements or wise decisions at a time when making deliberate choices that align with our higher good is the only thing that matters. In order to fulfill your true purpose you must move boldly in the direction of that purpose. Consider that each decision you make either takes you towards, or away from, that purpose.

Living out of alignment with your purpose can only move you towards thoughts and emotions that are on the southern hemisphere of the emotional spectrum. And those are all emotions that are ultimately ones of darkness. Light is the only thing that can overcome darkness. And to attract more light we must simply choose to do so. By this I do not mean you can simply apply positive thinking techniques to will yourself out of despair. No, I do not believe it works that way. Only action can get you to move away from one thing and towards another. If you are currently sitting down reading this book, close the book for a moment and use all your might to will yourself across the room. Think light happy thoughts about how you will feel sitting on the sofa opposite you. Visualize the soft carpet between your toes, the shift in lighting as you move away from the window. Can you smell the flowers in the vase on the other side of the room get stronger as you move to that side of the room? Sure you can. Now when you open your eyes are you sitting in the same space as before? Of course you are. Because you must take action. Thoughts and emotions *plus* action = results. Thoughts and emotions without actions equals, well, thoughts and emotions, better known as dreams. When we aren't taking action we are living in fantasy, and we are even further out of alignment with Source. To live a life of Design means living one of intention. It means trusting in the Divine and it means not being in a state of confusion. Which will require of you some action. It will require of you massive action.

In addition to quality execution, massive action will require of you honesty and accountability. We will dive into accountability later in the book, but I would like to address honesty right now. Seneca, in his *Letters from a Stoic* wrote:

"Choose someone whose way of life as well as words, and whose very face as mirroring the character that lies behind it, have won your approval. Be always pointing him out to yourself either as your guardian or as your model. This is a need, in my view, for someone as a standard against which our characters can measure themselves. Without a ruler to do it against you won't make the crooked straight."

We all need to have a coach or a mentor to help us stay honest. I invite you to identify who those people are in your life and to listen to them intently and apply what they say to your daily life. This doesn't have to be people you know or speak to. For me, I have many that I trust and respect. Some are personal friends and confidants. Others are leaders of business that I follow and listen to, dissect their podcasts and youtube channels and find ways to apply their philosophies to my own so I can intently move into massive action with thoughts of clarity.

It is important here to understand that thoughts are not true simply because they exist. You get to decide if they are true or not. You get to determine their nature. And if they are false thoughts, ones that take you away from Joy and Peace, then let them go. Consider for a moment some of the negative thoughts you have throughout the day. Do you recall consciously bringing those negative thoughts to your consciousness? More than likely not. Thoughts can be deliberate. They can also be, and often are, random and fleeting. Sometimes even confusing and dark. The fastest way I have learned to bring light to my thoughts, to move from confusion to understanding, is to simply let go of the thoughts that do not serve me. Laugh at their folly and the silliness of their falsehood. Whatever the root cause of your confusion, whatever emotional state you allow it to spiral you into, I invite you to combat that state with light. You can do this in multiple ways.

Explore the opportunities available to you and find the one that resonates best. I would recommend that you first move yourself into a place of gratitude. Take 90 seconds and shift your focus to three things within your life that you are currently grateful for. Put your energy into those things for 30 seconds each while just allowing the negative thoughts and emotions to drift off as you focus on the good that God has provided for you in this time and place. Perhaps take a moment then to write them down in a journal. This is a typical practice for me as a way to shift my energy. An additional way to get to a well lit space, in my experience, is to serve those around you. Shift your actions from serving yourself towards serving others. We must serve more to get more.

You can shift your mindset into one of service by selecting any one of numerous ways to serve another - call a friend and ask what they are up to, offer to support them if in any way you can. Simply listen and bring an ear of positivity to their current situation. Keep the focus on them and do not allow the conversation to drift to yourself. Looking for a friend in need? Go to your social media streams and I promise you within 5 minutes someone, somewhere will be complaining about something. Reach out and support them with your whole heart. Don't leave some positive meme or comment - really offer to connect with them.

And don't just commiserate with them about their issue. Offer them a solution, or help them see the silver lining. When you can inspire others to see light, you will shine brighter. An amazing spoken word artist, a poet, named Shane Koyczan, whom I admire greatly wrote "Some people just need a little more light than others, so make more." That's it, make more light. And when you do your own darkness will start to fade as well.

There are other tools available to move you away from confusion as well. It seems to me though they all sort of come back to the concept of gratitude. The Bible says you cannot serve two Masters (Matthew 6:24) It is also true that you cannot live in faith and fear at the same time. And you can not live in gratitude and suffering at the same time. The amazing thing is that, again, you get to choose your state of being.

It is vital that we get our emotional state to a place where it is confused less and less. Confusion breeds a lack of clarity. A lack of clarity sends us spiraling; putting our energy in numerous directions, looking for solutions to challenges that are based on assumption and may not even exist. This causes you to express this less focused energy in too many places. You are multitasking impossible tasks and chasing too many rabbits, and when we chase two rabbits, let alone imaginary ones, we catch none. This will always yield you poor results, and will rarely align you with living to your highest potential. A place of understanding brings clarity, clarity brings focus. Your search for understanding will be necessary in order to continue forward progress.

Ethan Nichtern is a senior teacher in the Shambhala Buddhist tradition, and the author of *The Road Home: A Contemporary Exploration of the Buddhist Path.* The following short passage is from Chapter 4 of that book, entitled *Being Human:*

> The key to being a warrior is being brave enough to repeatedly look honestly at your own heartmind, to be fearless enough to keep challenging your own negative views of who you are.

When we think of warriors we often think of those fighting for others, fighting for justice and putting themselves on the line for the greater good. I default to and rather prefer Ethan's description. The way of the warrior is one of courage, and bravery and vigor. To face confusion and anger, to truly overcome it, you must be a warrior. We do not give ourselves and our fellow warriors enough credit for the inner work that they do. A warrior is not only one who conquers, or masters another, but the one who can truly master himself.

This mastery of the warrior mentality also requires one to be vulnerable. We as a society often look at vulnerability as weakness. We put up walls much faster then we are able to take them down and we often put them up unnecessarily. We have been conditioned to believe that any sign of weakness will be our downfall. I think this is in large part to long standing patterns and schools of thought in parenting that suggest everyone needs to get a trophy. No one is allowed to lose and everyone must be a winner. Your feelings are somehow more important than reality. No.

In any conflict there will be one who will win, and one, if not many, who will lose. We cannot all be winners all the time. I actually prefer to shift my mindset here and have decided that I never lose. That is, I either win, or I learn.

In fact, reality is that I usually don't win. It really was as simple as deciding to shift the way I looked at losing and how I choose to process that 'loss' as learning. It is in that loss that I learn, because it is within that loss that I allow myself to be vulnerable; to look within and see where I have failed and where I need improvement. In order to grow and progress, to be a Warrior, you must embrace your vulnerability. In doing so you will need to find courage and grace. These are not signs of weakness but strength. To admit one's faults and to face them with clarity and determination requires one to be courageous. At no time in the history of man has one leapt into a circumstance of risk and fear without courage. And no one would say that a courageous person is a weak person.

Every man builds his world in his own image. He has the power to choose, but no power to escape the necessity of choice

Ayn Rand

So let's begin. And as we begin the real exploration here I want you to first understand that I freely admit that most of these ideas are not new. What you will read here you quite possibly have read, or have certainly heard some version of, before stumbling upon it here. If you continue down this road of human development, you will also more than likely hear many of these ideas presented again. Now, if this is your first foray into the category of what some call personal development then welcome to the club! It is certainly a large and diverse group that have chosen to take responsibility for their lives and their decisions over the course of time. I prefer to think of this journey as one of human development, because while this is your personal journey, we always leave a ripple everywhere we go. That ripple will without fail impact others. Your development, in any manner, will in fact, effect humanity, and so this is actually a journey of expansive human development, and one that I consider to be philosophically rooted.

This journey is certainly personal to you, and each of our journeys will also be singularly specific to us. No matter how personal this is however, it is important to always be mindful that this is a process affecting all. I hope you enjoy the ideas held within these pages as you continue and that they expand your journey. I also want to be clear in the intention: this book will not fix you. I have no degree that says I am qualified to repair damaged goods and if you are looking for clear and concise answers you may well be disappointed. In fact, this book will hopefully leave you with more questions than answers. It will, of done right, give you pause to sit with yourself and find the cracks you need to repair. Read that part again … you will need to be the one fixing yourself.

Each of you that embark from here will gain different insights and knowledge and each of you will have different ideas and actionable items that resonate with you on your own frequency. I hope that by sharing with you my own journey and individual perspective and discussing these topics through the lens with which I have come to view the world I can shed some new light on them. A view from a different angle perhaps, that will help you to choose different; if that is what you want. Notice I didn't use the word *better*? I won't pretend to know what is good, better, or best for you. We most likely have never met and it would be insanely presumptuous of me to tell you what is best for you. It has been said that sometimes you will need to say a thing 100 times before the other person hears it. Perhaps someone has said these things to you 99 times already, and now you are ready to truly hear them for the first time.

A few years ago someone posed a relatively, or so I thought at the time, innocuous question to me:

"Are you living your life by design or by default?"

I believe we are all creators, if not at least co-creators. I have been drawing, writing, painting and designing spaces and ideas for as long as I can remember. And since I was actively working as a professional Designer at the time, having earned a bachelor's degree in Interior Design, I thought, 'What kind of question is that? By design? Of course?!?!'

Yet, when I really considered the implications of what that question meant I quickly realized that perhaps I was, in fact, living my life by default. Not even perhaps, but certainly. I mean, there were things that my wife and I had planned out: kids, college, careers, etc. But if I am being honest with you about where we were at in 2006 I would be lying if I told you we were 'on track'. Or at least I wasn't. I was working two jobs, we were barely able to make ends meet most months and while I would have bragged then about having had my act together, now I wasn't so sure.

As a father and husband I began to understand that our current trajectory was just plain unacceptable. It occurred to me that as a father and a husband anything done by default seemed to be irresponsible at best. Not only were there people depending on me, but these were people that looked at me to really know what I was doing. Whether that was my wife and kids, or colleagues I worked with and the employees who I managed. It seemed to me upon further review that I had somehow never looked at my life in terms of who, or what, was in control. It was obvious at that time that I could no longer afford to just sort of float along.

As discussed earlier, I had grown up in a household that was vacant of tools with which to manage the dynamics of the people within it. That upbringing was certainly one of default, so I had seen with my own eyes what a life by default looked like. Was that really what I wanted for my family? Had that brought me happiness and prosperity? It was at this time that I had decided that something had to change. But what? Where does one even begin to shift the decades of ones own life story, or the generations of family history and the lifetime of labels and identity that we all cling to? It didn't take long for me to determine that if things were going to change, I was going to have to change something. And that something was *me*.

And so it began. I knew what it meant to create something from nothing. I knew what it was like to take a blank page, a blank room, or an empty lot and create a drawing or a story, or a usable and often visually appealing space out of virtually nothing. So how hard could it be to do that with myself? How hard could it be to view the life I had as a blank slate? Well, apparently pretty damn hard. I wasn't a blank slate. I wasn't new and fresh and without beliefs and experiences and neither are you. Redefining who I was and how I moved about the world meant taking the things I knew about creating and revisiting them. I was going to have to implement what Buddhists call

Beginner's Mind. This was going to have to be a collaboration. One between God, the old me, and the new me. This was going to have to be a team effort. And while I enjoy collaboration, I like to lead. I had let enough of those other people tell me what to do in the past. I let other people tell me how the real world worked before and look where that got me. Obviously they were clearly off base, right? So not only was there some new ideas about what it meant to create that I was going to have to learn, but it sounded like I was also going to have to learn how to trust again. Looking at the big picture it seemed obvious to me that I had two choices, and maybe this will sound familiar to you:

> *Option 1* - Keep doing what I had been doing and pray real hard that I catch a break
>
> OR
>
> *Option 2* - Start listening to and collaborating with different people. People who were living the life I wanted. If they had it maybe I could just do what they did too.

Option Two seemed like a viable option, and it sort of seemed like the only option, considering the scant tools I was given by my upbringing. I decided it was time to really start designing the life I wanted. I decided it was time to co-create with mentors and coaches, to trust in the journey, and finally, to get some help.

So what does it mean to live by design or by default? Because I tend to operate from the place that words have meaning, let's look at the meanings of those two words:

Default: *a selection made usually **automatically or without active consideration** due to a lack of viable alternative.*
Synonyms: *blunder, error, miss, neglect*

Design: *a method **worked out in advance** for achieving some objective.*
Synonyms: *game plan, master plan, road map*

A selection made automatically without active consideration due to a lack of (or perceived lack of) a viable alternative. Seems like laziness to me, or maybe complacency is a better word. And when I think of the millions of people who are truly living their life by default I do not think of lazy people. How many of us know truly lazy people? That description certainly doesn't fit the majority of the people I know. The majority of the people I knew then, and many of the people I still know today, live lives by default. So if it wasn't laziness that was driving that force, what was it? Yes, I think complacency is the right word here. Complacency is defined as a feeling of smug or uncritical satisfaction with oneself or one's achievements. Yeah, that sounds like a tremendous amount of the people I know. It sounds like me before this journey. And I think if you were to really dig down, look in the mirror, or have some honest conversations with your closest friends you would see that most people are content to 'get by'. Even those who have some level of accomplishment aren't impassioned by it. They are probably more in alignment with a feeling of uncritical satisfaction.

John Yniques, Grouchy John Nation

'Grouchy' John has the most genuine smile of just about any guy I know. He founded Grouchy John's Coffee with his good friend JJ Wylie back in 2010 at a local music, food and art festival held in Las Vegas, NV called First Friday. That first night, as he tells it, "we had a fold out table, a little espresso machine, a 20 year old Mr. Coffee coffee maker, and no idea what the hell we were doing." What John and JJ didn't realize then was that night was life changing for them in almost too many ways to count. John continues "It only took the great recession and almost 15 years of working for other people in a corporate environment to realize that I needed to create my own job and that I should have been running my own business all along." What he came to realize that night is that he didn't need to work for someone else, and that he could build something on his own. What he realized was that he *had* to take the risk. Part of the reason why John's story made it's way into this chapter is this part of his journey that he shared with me, "After that night I stopped looking for another job and starting learning how to create, operate, and build something I could call my own. I was all in on this venture. I cashed out all my retirement accounts, bought a trailer that we then converted into a mobile coffee trailer, along with new upgraded coffee equipment, and started looking for gigs around town." John made a choice. A choice to stop allowing someone else to make decisions for him, and to take control of his situation. They knew it would be work. They started out slow and there would be times where these guys would be out all day and only make $100. John continued to share the purpose for his journey. "I knew we were putting our heart and souls into everything we served and when I would see somebody enjoying a latte or cappuccino that I made, it would keep me going. You see, not only did I make the drink, I *chose* the espresso that would go in the drink, I learned how to steam the milk perfectly for enjoyment, I *chose* the espresso machine, and the type of water that was used. About the only things we don't do is pick and roast the beans. But when you do all that and see someone smile after they have a sip, it is pretty damn satisfying."

As this book comes to print it will be 7 years since that first night at First Friday. Grouchy John's still operates the little trailer almost on a daily basis but it now also has two brick and mortar shops and a second, larger coffee truck that is in constant use, with over 50 employees and yearly sales of over $1 million. When asked if he ever doubts his decision to leave the corporate world and spread his wings John relies quickly "To say I don't doubt my decision everyday since that first night would be wrong. What I don't doubt is that I am 10 times happier right now than I ever was working for someone else. I do know that doing it the way I did it may not for everybody. I wasn't married, I don't have kids, and I did have something saved up to be able to take this risk. But if you can build something for yourself and are willing to make the choice, I highly suggest doing it."

This is why we hear stories, like that of Grouchy John, of the successful businessman who leaves his high paying corporate job to go surf full time or paint happy little trees, or to make coffee and serve others, and we typically root for that guy. We rarely see the guy in the three piece suit working and achieving at a high 'socially acceptable' level and want to be that guy. We may want his money, but we don't want to sacrifice what he sacrifices to get it because deep down we know that guy isn't happy.

A quick story if I may. My wife and I homeschool our kids (a result of a designed life that we will get into later). Most of my oldest sons friends however are not. He is our most social child and he spends a reasonable amount of time outside of the home at the skatepark, work, or enjoying the outdoors. So most of the kids his age he hangs out with are publicly educated teens at this point. One evening he had two of his skatepark friends over to the house and we invited them to stay for dinner. Our family typically has dinner together and with 7 kids that makes for quite the affair, adding 2 more to the table is hardly noticeable. Over the course of the meal their futures came up. Would they be going to college? What are they thinking about as careers? Families? Would they stay here in Colorado or be going off to the see the world?

I was looking forward to hearing all about their future plans. As it turns out, they were much less excited. In fact the idea of a future seemed almost depressing to them.

"Well, I think I want to be a mechanic" one declared.

"Oh, do you enjoy working on cars?" I asked.

"I guess. It's what my Dad does, so I guess that's what I'll do. And my grades kinda suck so college seems like a bust" was his matter of fact response. He didn't seem to even think that there were other options. And he certainly wasn't displaying any excitement about his chosen career path.

The other young man at the table chimed in, almost to save his friend "I want to work in the medical field. I think I am going to do Xray or something like that. They make good money"

"Yes, Xray technicians can make a good living" I agreed. "Are you concerned at all about the radiation though? I don't know if I would want to be around that all the time"

"Well, yeah, I guess it's risky. But as long as I can make enough to get by, it's worth it!" he responded.

"Oh, is that enough though? To just get by?" I followed up with.

"Oh yeah, most of us right now, we know everything's a mess. Getting by is better than most. I'd be happy with that for sure." And with that the conversation turned to other things.

I sat there quietly finishing my meal and contemplating those words. 'Getting by is better than most'. Getting by is nearly the definition of default isn't it? It certainly sounds like 'without active consideration' to me. And yet, here was a young man that was actively considering exactly that, just getting by. I'd like to chalk the attitudes of these young men up to their age, or the daunting idea of planning a future at 17. The reality is though that upon further investigation, many, far too many, of the people I've had the courage to ask, are content with getting by, living their life by default.

This came up again recently when my wife and I were watching an episode of the television show Undercover Boss. In case you aren't familiar, this show's premise is that a CEO or business owner will go undercover and work as a line level employee to see how the company is really doing. It is a favorite show of ours. I think we love it because at the end the undercover boss reveals himself to the employees and the ones he is more intimate with get huge life changing rewards. A new car for the student who walks or rides his bike to and from school and work. A mortgage paid off or a family vacation for the cashier who is helping parents pay the bills after some medical tragedy. Those sort of grab a tissue and remember humans are basically good to one another type of moments.

In this one particular episode there was a young man that really impressed the CEO. When the big reveal came the CEO wanted to do something nice for the employee and asked him "if you could do anything, what would it be? What are you really passionate about?" And the young man's response sums up for me the way we have been conditioned to think now. "Well, if I am being realistic, I'd like to…." and I don't remember the rest of his answer. It didn't matter because in my head I was screaming "why be realistic?!!!?" Being 'realistic' does not sound joy filled.

I know I do not want what others deem for me as realistic and I hope that you do not want that either.

In the event that you were willing to accept the status quo before, it is my hope that you are no longer willing to accept such a fate now. Hopefully you are ready to live a life by design, to devise a road map that is of a life of abundance. Abundance that is somewhat worked out in advance. I hope that this is why you picked up this book. Or at least by now that you are interested enough to continue. A life of Design seems much more satisfying, yes? Strategized and thought out. Yes, that seems more like the purposeful choice to me. As it turns out many of us are living our life by default. Not because we choose to, but because we don't know how to choose different.

I do not believe that God's intention was for you to suffer a life of complacency. I do not believe that we are here simply to float along and take what comes our way without the ability to co-create. I do not believe that there is a lack of viable alternatives. If this were the case there would be no light bulb, no steam engine, no iphone or NETFLIX. Every day someone, somewhere, is choosing to not accept what is placed in front of them and to put forth ideas that will forever imprint our society. As a matter of fact, regardless of your conscious decision to do so or not, your life is doing the same thing. You are leaving a ripple, this massive imprint.

The only thing left for you to decide is what will that imprint be? Will it be something you desire it to be, or will it just be? To the innovators and creators in this world, will everyone of them be successful? It is unlikely. Something will get in the way. But many will break through. What is it that set's *them* apart? The ones who will succeed. What is it in the DNA of those who shift the dynamics of society so drastically that we remember their names and take a day off from work in their honor? I believe it is choices. I believe they know how to choose differently than most. And I believe that they know that to do otherwise is a death sentence.

In philosophy there are two primary ideologies, Empiricism, also know as the Blank Slate, and Innatism. My understanding of the first posits that we are all born a blank slate, and that everything we come to know is somehow a learned condition. We are essentially born free and un-imprinted. Everything we know is taught, not just the names of trees, animals, birds and the like, but also love, anger, jealousy, and the difference between right and wrong. John Locke, a British philosopher, is widely considered the founder of modern empiricism, and is famously attributed with holding the proposition that the human mind is a "blank tablet", or what Locke called a "white paper". This is where the experiences derived from sense impressions over time as a person's life proceeds are written.

Innatism refers to the philosophy of Plato and Descartes, who presented the idea that God, or a Higher Power, or process, placed innate ideas and principles within the human psyche. This would suggest that we are born with some level of innate knowledge or understanding, at the very least an ideology; an instinctual knowing of the difference between right and wrong. Now I am confident that I am over simplifying these two concepts, considering the decades of conversation and the volumes of books written about the pros and cons of each. It is not my intent to get into a philosophical debate about the merits of the two positions. You are more than welcome to delve into that subject on your own, and I invite you to do so. However, for the purposes of this journey, I do believe that there is some truth in both concepts.

Much, but perhaps not all of what we 'know' is a learned behavior or belief, therefore empirical in nature. Not everything though. There are basic survival instincts that are present such as fight, flight or freeze. We know when we need to eat, we know when to seek shelter and to protect ourselves from the elements, and therefore innate.

Have you ever watched babies interact at a very young age? it is quite evident that love and kindness, compassion and empathy are innate feelings exhibited without impunity. Or perhaps you have been in the unique position to be present at the birth of a child. In natural birth there is an experience called the breast crawl. Once the child is born, and often before mother and child are separated from the umbilical cord, the seconds old child is placed on the mothers torso or chest and he or she will innately wiggle and squirm until it finds the mothers breast, latching on and nursing. No one has taught them to do this. No one has explained where the source of nutrition is. They just know. It is hard wired into their little minds. Taking this concept even further, I am certain that we are all brought on to this planet with a mission, or a purpose, and with very unique personalities designed and molded to carry out that purpose. And while all the intricacies of that personality may not have been defined yet, the core dynamics are in place from birth, if not before. If we can heighten our awareness enough and we can commit to removing the clutter and noise we are surrounded with we can achieve our purpose more easily than others.

Take identical twins as another example, born of the same DNA, under the same roof, eating the same food and sharing an almost identical experience. Immediately you'll notice that they are nearly identical in size and shape, eye color, hair color, personality traits and many other visible metrics. And yet, they are easily identifiable to those who spend time with them because they are individually unique. Unique in numerous intangible ways and often with differing passions and motivations.

Then we can look at all of the various beliefs that people hold; religion, politics, ethical and social conditions, cultural and socio-economic drivers and why and how those came to be. The value of a dollar, the importance of saving, the seemingly insurmountable division so prevalent in our society today. These are all learned behaviors and ideologies. Beliefs and concepts that are derived from stimuli, experience, deduction and reasoning, or perhaps a lack thereof. These are not innate, nor are they a part of our psyche when we are brought into this world. So if we can agree that somewhere, on some level, that both Empiricism and Innatism hold some truth, then we can begin to talk about the large and small ripples we create due to the decisions we make. We can begin to realize and bring understanding to the fact that we are indeed co-creators in this existence!

This is the foundation that the remainder of this conversation is to be taken from. If this is a place you believe doesn't exist then now is the time to close the book and use it as a coaster (we designed it with a beautiful cover in case that suits you better).

And if you choose to carry on from here then the first thing to do is accept that everything else from here on out will be your fault.

chapter three
THE PROBLEM IS PROBABLY YOU
(seriously, it really is)

You are the way you are because that's the way you want to be. If you really wanted to be any different, you would be in the process of changing right now.

Fred Smith, Founder, Federal Express

With this newly defined perspective it then becomes vitally important that you also understand that everything you are experiencing is the result of the mostly conscious, and sometimes subconscious, decisions that you have made, and that you are still making today. While this book is about living by design, or what is also referred to as living with intention, the reality is that every one of us is already living with intention. Unfortunately it is largely an unexamined, subconscious intention and the large majority of people are actually living not with intention, but *within tension*. The question we must ask ourselves and commit to resolving is this: which one of those two circumstances will you choose to be in? And we need to begin to resolve it, and to prevent it in the future, consciously.

While we may not always choose to see and hear what fills our minds, we do choose what we do with it, or how we respond. In that same ideal, there is an inordinate amount of data that we do choose: the music we listen to, the television we watch, the books we read, the people we associate with and the sources of our education are primarily, especially in adulthood, ours to determine. This will be a particularly important distinction moving forward, *'that which is occurring in adulthood'*.

Clearly, most adolescents and certainly children are at the mercy of their caretakers to a much greater extent than an adult who has ventured out into the world and is now on their own with regard to the hundreds of day to day choices that are made for them. However, adolescents do have the ability to choose how they respond to the stimuli they receive, which is why you can have two siblings in nearly identical situations resulting in such different people. They may be under the same constraints, but they choose to respond in different manners. Taking that into consideration, regardless of your living situation, if you are of the age of 18 or above, you are solely responsible for you, and certainly more often than not we get to choose what goes into our heads. All too often we are not, however, doing so by design. We have allowed input that does not serve us to enter the library.

We have lined the shelves with too much nonsense.

Have you ever been in the middle of a television show, a movie or a song, and said to yourself 'why am I watching/listening to this?' How often do you actually change the input though? How often do you sit there in some relative form of frustration or apathy, maybe even self disgust, as you and whatever mindless entertainment you're participating in fall deeper into a spiral of degradation? This is a choice that you have. To sit and continue to participate in that which clearly doesn't serve you or to move on to something better, or at the very least, different.

My wife, Keri, is a master of this. If she doesn't like the music I am listening to, sorry Chris Cornell, she changes the station. Or leaves the room. Whether it is television or music, any stimulus that she cannot obviously control, she does not partake in it if it lowers her energy and she is able to without offending the other party. This goes for people in our lives as well. We all have people that we have no business being around. The negativity, bickering and downward outlook on life is not necessary. And she does not tolerate it. The first time Keri got up and left the room when I put on Soundgarden I remember feeling hurt. I took it very personally. I was offended that she didn't want to spend time with *me*. Upon further examination and after a bit of self development I have come to realize that it literally has nothing to do with me. While the teen angst of the grunge area still resonates with me deeply, it just isn't her thing for the most part. And since it lowers her vibration it isn't given the space to be within that vibration.

Don't get me wrong. If I may brag on my amazing wife for a moment, I will tell you that there aren't many in the world that shine brighter than her. And Keri's occasional distaste for my loud music or an acquaintances poor attitude is hardly met with anything other than healthy boundaries wrapped in genuine love and light. Many of us today though do not understand what a healthy boundary is. For a long time I could count myself in that group as well.

Conceivably it is your own life that seems to be lowering your energy. Are the circumstances surrounding your current place in this existence within the category of stimulus that you'd rather not be receiving? Perhaps you are choosing to numb your internal pain with senseless noise and other vapid content that may or may not make you feel slightly better, but certainly helps you forget reality. When you are indeed forced to look in the mirror, evaluate how you spend your time and why - do you spend hours a day on Facebook, twitter, SnapChat or Instagram comparing your real life self to the online persona of your 'friends' and wondering why your thoughtful, enigmatic post about this or that got only a handful of likes or hearts, while the photo of your key lime pie is somehow trending on twitter? Or worse still, it may be that you choose to numb those feelings with medication, or alcohol, or otherwise dysfunctional relationships. More than likely if this is the current state of affairs that make up your current reality then it is not the result of you saying, "Yes! This is where I want my life to be."

Certainly you didn't sit down after graduation and say to your parents:

> "Hey Mom & Dad, I am really looking forward to busting my ass in college and digging myself into debt so that I can be miserable from now until 65

or so, hoping that when I retire, my future children, who I hope don't hate me, can take care of me until I keel over and die. But, hey, at least there's facebook."

You may laugh at this idea but the harsh reality is that it is widely believed that out of 100 people who start working at the age of 25, by the age of 65 or so, approximately one will be wealthy, another four will have enough money to retire, about 63 will depend on social security or charity of some sort and the remaining 29 will be deceased or relatively close to it. Let that potentiality sink in for a minute. I'm sure most of you aren't even surprised a little by those numbers. Picture your family and friends, the sphere of influence you have currently surrounded yourself with. Can you pick out the people who fall into those given areas? Given those exciting figures I refuse to believe this has all been happening to us on a social level consciously.

Feasibly the harshest reality we all must accept though is that we are in fact exactly where we have chosen to be. Your current living situation, your current income, your current relationships. Regardless of success or failure, your current level of happiness can all be traced to what you have chosen, or not chosen, to do. Many have argued this point with me in the past only to discover upon reflection that this is an inescapable truth. You took the job, you moved in with that loser, you chose to go to the bar and get hammered, you decided to dodge the bill collector. There's a reason you are looking for a way to choose different.

And yet, if you take a look at your social media feeds and the headline news for the next week there is a frightening pattern that has emerged. You will soon begin to recognize how often people are placing the blame in our culture for their own behavior on that of others. How many times do you see someone say 'So and so made me do this or feel this'? 'Well if hadn't have said or done that I wouldn't have been forced to do the other thing!' There is even a popular song at the moment titled 'Look What You Made Me Do' by Taylor Swift. At the time I am writing this it is number 2 on the charts. Look what you made me do.....this is the message we are sending our young women and men through cultural messaging. You have power over me to manage my behavior. Certainly people have influence on us. But we need to be crystal clear that no one has influence over us unless we allow them to have it. Our actions are ours regardless of what another person does to encourage, incite or influence us.

With this in mind, I'd like to invite you to consider a few things about how you've come to make these decisions in the past:

- How did you come to those decisions; what resources were you able to pull from?
- Are those resources sound, tested and rooted in honesty; are they coming from a place meant to bring you joy?
- Are they stable resources that have supported you kindly in the past?
- Did you make conscious choices or did you operate from a place where the perceived lack of viable options was all too real and so the non-choice was your choice?

Well, perhaps at the time, what you thought to be real was as real as anything really is. Which is to say that reality is often just your perception of it. In spite of the how, what we can say is that you ended up here today. You ended up with this book in your hands, having a conversation about choices, how they effect your reality, and potentially how to make different, perhaps even better ones. At the very least I hope that by sharing my own experiences and discoveries you too will find it necessary to assume responsibility for the decisions you have made and view their results with less confusion and more opportunity.

When I first entered into this journey of accountability and choosing different I assure you it made the hair on the back of my neck stand up and I may or may not have broken into a bit of a sweat. At that time in my life my marriage was in jeopardy, I was violent and angry, with both my children and the people around me in general. My overall career path was shaky and to say that I lacked clear direction would be the understatement of understatements. I was pretty clearly and vocally not happy with my situation, perhaps miserable would be a better way to describe it, and at the same time I was not wanting to take full ownership of it. To be honest, I wasn't really interested in taking *any* ownership of it. Most people I have had the opportunity to have face to face conversations with regarding them taking ownership of their own bullshit aren't really excited about the idea either. And yet, at some point we are all faced with this reality, regardless of whether we see it coming or not. I promise you if it hasn't happened to you yet, it will. It may be on your death bed, in the waning moments of your life, but at some point you will be forced to see the totality of your life's decisions. It seems to me that we would rather face those decisions now, at a time when we have the physical and mental strength to make broad and lasting change. The alternative would be facing those circumstances in the last moments of your life, be it days, months or years, where perhaps the frailty of old age has set in and prevents you from making the important changes you could have made and regret overwhelms your thoughts?

You see, we all make choices every day. This morning you woke up, presumably at the sound of an alarm clock, possibly after numerous dances with a snooze button. Took a shower, brushed your teeth, maybe did your makeup and hair, or shaved your face, then got dressed and moved on to having your coffee, getting breakfast ready, maybe getting the kids off to school. That's about three dozen decisions in the span of an hour. And there's probably another few dozen in there we left out, like what to wear, what to eat, how to do your hair blah, blah, blah. If I was to go over every single decision we make in a day this would be a 1200 page book and you'd be bored to tears reading it. In fact, various sources that have taken the time to actually analyze this sort of thing put the adult decision making number at around 35,000 a day! For perspective that is about 24 decisions every minute, or 1 every 2.5 seconds. How many of those do you really have to consciously plan in order to execute? Relatively speaking, that number is probably pretty low.

Many of our day to day decisions become habit after time. The neural pathways in our brain are developed over time and most of those activities occur almost subconsciously as we move about the environment in which we live. So thousands of those decisions are made in a nano second with relatively little visible impact on the outcome of your life and even less consideration of those impacts. And yet each of those outcomes has a profound effect on the remainder of our day, and often times they do actually have a profound impact on the balance of your world. Often times we think that the results of our choices are happening to us and not for us, or that they are of little to no significance. You work where you work because you applied there. You live where you live because you signed the lease. You live with, or don't live with, the people you do, or don't, because that's how it is. I often hear people say, "Well, I didn't have a choice." Reflect for a moment on the conversations you have had with your friends where that response has come up. How many times does someone tell you they did the thing they did because they didn't have a choice? Or better yet, how many times have you said that about your own various situations? William James, American philosopher and psychologist said "When you have to make a choice and don't make it, that is in itself a choice." Consider these scenarios for a moment:

I would rather be living with my estranged wife and kids, but she kicked me out. I had no choice in that. Why would I not want to be with my kids?

I totally want to get a new job, but it's just not doable since I don't have reliable transportation.

I have this awesome business idea that I know will make millions. If only I had the money or resources to achieve it. It's never going to happen.

I can't go to the gym because it's expensive and too far away, and I don't really have time to since I have to get to work and get kids to school

My current income only allows me to live in this zip code, this neighborhood or this city. I'd love to live in Austin, TX or Portland, OR, but I just can't.

Does any of that sound familiar? Perhaps not these specific scenarios, or maybe not even in your life currently, but for someone, and at sometime, these examples are most likely ones you can relate to on some level. If it does resonate with you then the first question to ask yourself is about any of the presented circumstances is this - is this absolutely true? Take any of the above statements that apply to you, or someone you know, and ask yourself "Is this true" and if you are honest with yourself you will discover that it most likely is not. When we assign the blame to someone else for our situation, or the result of our choices, we are giving away our power as creators and we are choosing to play the role of the victim. You are only a victim if you choose to be. Brené Brown defines blame as simply the discharging of pain and discomfort. Of course it makes sense that we would want to discharge pain and discomfort. Our brains are wired to protect us, so it makes sense biologically. But we aren't living under Neanderthal conditions any longer and perhaps it is time that we dig into our pain and discomfort a bit more and examine where it is really sprouting from. I would argue that we are able to sit with it, learn to be brave and to challenge it head on.

You want to live with your estranged wife and kids but she kicked you out. That wasn't a random decision she made, nor one that just popped out one day. More than likely that was the result of your combined decisions about how you navigated that relationship. Whatever expectations she or you had about how marriage was supposed to work, one, or both of you, chose to do things your own way; chose not to compromise and resolve your challenges together. And in the end the relationship crumbles. It isn't a random circumstance and you aren't a victim here. You are a co-creator of that experience, however challenging that may be to hear.

You really want to get out of this dead end, minimum wage and thankless job. And it just isn't possible because you can barely afford gas, and your car breaks down too often. Sure, some things are hard. Almost anything worth doing is hard. Taking night classes to expand your skills is an investment in time and most likely some money. Which means maybe not driving and taking public transit, or moving closer to work and walking a few days a week. Or every day. Or perhaps this job can become a career if you chose to get there early and stay late instead of rushing home to catch Game of Thrones or Monday Night Football. The choices are yours to make. If the job doesn't fuel your passion, then move on when the time is appropriate or change your point of view on it. See it as a means to an end while you work toward the thing you want most. But do so with a happy heart.

Whether you choose to like it or not, we all must accept trade-offs in order to move forward. If you had a roommate could you afford a nicer neighborhood? A better residence? What would living in a nicer, or just different neighborhood mean for you? While you may currently have a job, and it's working 'just for now', do you have the ability to look for and obtain something better? As we talked about earlier, we all make multiple decisions every day. From what we eat to what we wear to what we think. Some of these are conscious decisions that take a few moments thought. Some are major decisions that takes deep thought, conversation and analyzing the pros and cons. These are all decisions nonetheless and while we can accept responsibility for the small ones that don't necessarily reflect poorly on us, we seem to forget our role in the larger, more egregious ones.

This may be where we get into trouble. It is here in that space of the minor decision making, what I call 'micro-decisions', that a slow but definitive cumulative effect takes place. These are all the little things that we almost, and often times in our minds, justify as inconsequential. The overwhelming truth is that there are no inconsequential decisions or actions. Everything leaves a ripple.

Newton's third law of motion: *For every action there is an equal and opposite reaction*

In this context it means that literally nothing is inconsequential. For every thought, idea and emotion you have there is a push/pull that will occur. How you manage, or react to these movements in your mind will determine the decisions you make; how quickly, how effectively and how deliberately. Some of these choices exist in the macro and other decisions, certainly the silent majority if you will, are micro. What I have discovered is that we often times give great care

and consideration when undertaking the macro
decisions and very little of the same attention to that
of the micro.

Macro decisions are easy to identify and the results
are very often intense. These consist of the life altering
decisions that we are highly aware of - moving,
changing jobs, having kids, buying a new car. Many of
us will carefully weigh the pros and cons, we will
analyze the data and most importantly we will very
likely take our time. We rarely get in the car, drive
down to the car dealership and just drop $30,000 or
more on a new automobile without a test drive,
reading numerous reviews, or consulting our friends
and family first. We know that there is a visible,
tangible effect these decisions will have and so we
tend to take more care with how we make them. More
often than not this allows us to have a certain level of
comfort and satisfaction with our decision making.

It is within the realm of the micro decisions that we
make that we most often get into trouble. It is those
innumerable micro decisions that we typically make by
default.

So what do we do to make that shift? To do this, and
we will discuss this later in the book, we must
learn awareness. Awareness of the impact our choices
make, a mindfulness of the reality that we are in fact
leaving a ripple with each choice. We must learn to
execute our decisions from a higher place of
understanding, and I believe it to be a place of service.
If we know our decisions have a greater impact then
we have a responsibility to our fellow humans to make
better choices. We owe it to each other to energize
those around us, to empower them and not to

disempower them. We must have clarity in what we are doing and why we are doing it. We must be willing to show up recognizing our actions and decisions as ours. We must choose to find awareness in what we have done in the past, and if it isn't serving us to our highest good, and therefore rippling out love and light, we must choose to change our story.

To illustrate how much even the smallest miscue can affect things, let's look to something most of us have participated in at least once - manned flight. This is a prime example of where precision and care is an absolute must. I was astounded to learn that when flying an airplane the slightest error in course can cause catastrophic effects. In fact, here are some amazing statistics about flying an airplane that veers just one degree off course:

- By being just one degree off course, you will miss your destination by 92 feet for every mile that you fly.
- For every 60 miles you fly, you will miss your target by one mile.
- Flying around the equator will land you almost 500 miles off target.
- Flying from LAX to JFK will put you nearly 50 miles off course. Which by the way drops you into the ocean. Perhaps this is why your seat will double as a flotation device.

Clearly in the course of manned flight there have been miscalculations. This is where the term course correction comes from. When in the course of action you determine you are off course, you must correct your path of travel. We do this by analyzing our current path, determining where we want to be and creating an alternative plan to get us back on track. Again, this concept typically seems to be applied to the macro, flight, naval travel, corporate business etc. Why then are we hesitant to apply this concept to our own lives? This is the master of all journeys. Why is it that we too often choose not to course correct our lives until it is too late, if at all? I find it to be completely reasonable to apply these same mathematics to the trajectory of our lives when we consider how integrated mathematics is into our daily lives, and into the world around us. Some have successfully argued that the universe is math, and therefore so are you and I.

There is another, very similar, mathematical concept that may resonate with you even more, and is greatly detailed in the book by Jeff Olson, *The Slight Edge*. In *The Slight Edge* he speaks to that variable difference between those who have achieved great success and those who have not.

One of the concepts within the book is this: If you were to improve yourself a mere .003 percent each day, or 3/10 of one percent, you would improve 100 percent over the course of one year. Consider a .003 percent increase tomorrow over today, and the next day and the next. Imagine running 100 yards today. Perhaps that seems impossible for you, perhaps that seem's easy. But for the sake of illustration we'll use that figure.

You did it, you ran 100 yards full tilt, and on average you would burn about 50 calories. The next day you would run the same 100 yards + .003% more, or one additional yard. How ridiculously easy is that to add! After the course of a year you would be running 200 yards. An increased improvement of 100%. The second year, you would improve 100 percent over the first. The third year, 100 percent over the second and so on. And the fourth year, you're running almost a mile. Now it seems obvious that in this scenario the numbers seem small, and in fact you could easily go from running 100 yards to a mile in under a year.

However, let's look at the percentages here. By the end of year five, and by simply improving 3/10 of one percent each day you will have multiplied your value, your skills, and the results you accomplished by 1600 percent. You have the ability to change. You have the free will to choose. You can choose to add the .003% day after day. You can look at the current course, identify whether it suits you and your highest good, and determine to stay on course or you can choose to course correct. Eliminate the 1 degree off course you have been on and get back into a deliberate, purpose driven life. You are currently where you are because you have chosen to be there. Now you can decide to choose differently.

I have faced it... A life wasted,...
I'm never going back again.
I escaped it... A life wasted...
I'm never going back again.
Having tasted... A life wasted...
I'm never going back again

lyrics by Eddie Vedder

Believe - Decide - Execute. Nearly everything I have learned so far boils down to these three primary choices: Believe you can, Decide to do so, Execute the plan. Move into Action. You decide. You either decide to give up, and that's a decision, or you decide to press forward, and that's a decision. You decide *how* to move forward, *when* to get started and *where* to put your energy. Money, status, occupation. These things do not define you any more or less than any other label defines you. We use words to communicate ideas and concepts so that we can understand one another. I believe we have taken that need to communicate too far and have allowed these words to become defining characteristics that in reality are interpreted in various ways by everyone. These characteristics certainly have value, and consequence, and they certainly exist in so far as you perceive them, but that perception is determined by the individual. As such, you get to determine the value. And the value you determine may be different for you than for another person. You get to decide if these experiences, and these labels, will empower or disempower you. You get to decide if it is just a part of your journey, or allow it to be the thing that defines who you are.

"The ability to choose cannot be taken away - it can only be forgotten." Greg McKeown writes in his book *Essentialism, The Desired Pursuit of Less*. It is a truth that reinforces the reality and the importance of deliberate choices. This is an opportunity for you to claim your personal power. Will you exercise your ability to choose or will you forget that it exists?

Another truth, although one that is under debate as to where it generated from so I cannot properly credit it to any one person, is this:

> "Between stimulus and response, there is a space. In that space lies our freedom and power to choose our response. In our response lies our growth and our freedom"
>
> *Author Unknown*

That space between stimulus and response is where your power of choice, a power you have whether you claim it or not, lives. And it doesn't die until you take your last breath. You will always have a space between stimulus and response and you will always have the freedom and the power to choose. Certainly there are constraints that may limit your choices, and the space between stimulus and response may be shorter at times and longer at others. The universal truth remains that the space exists, will always exist, and it is yours to master.

A great example of this, and one that is cited regularly in conversations around choice and free will, is The Stanford Prison Experiment. The Stanford Prison Experiment was a psychological experiment performed by Stanford University in 1971. A group of researchers, led by Philip Zimbardo, who at the time was a psychology professor, used college students to investigate the causes of conflict between military guards and prisoners at the request, and funding, of the US Office of Naval Research. The study has become widely known and is a classic study on the effects, primarily psychological, of imprisonment.

In this experiment one group of college students was designated as 'jailers' and one was designated as 'jailed'.

The participants of the experiment adapted to their roles well beyond Zimbardo's expectations, as the guards enforced authoritarian measures and ultimately subjected some of the prisoners to psychological torture. Many of the prisoners passively accepted psychological abuse and, at the request of the guards, readily harassed the other prisoners who attempted to prevent it. The experiment even affected Zimbardo himself, who, in his role as the superintendent, permitted the abuse to continue. Two of the prisoners quit the experiment early, and the entire experiment was abruptly stopped after only six days, due largely because of the objections of participating facilitators. Certain portions of the experiment were filmed, and excerpts of footage are publicly available, including a film produced in 2015.

The participants in this experiment believed they were their designated roles, the jailer or the jailed. They made a decision to play the part, to act as if, and then they executed the duties of their designated roles. In doing so they allowed the labels placed upon them to dictate their actions, and to define them. Their preconceived ideas of what a person in that role would do, or how they would behave, is the persona they chose to adopt. In doing so they made numerous, sometimes simultaneous, micro-decisions that were admittedly not in alignment with their true personality. Nor were they in alignment with what we would consider to be morally acceptable treatment of other human beings. Had certain individuals that were involved not had the presence of mind to intervene, irreparable damage may have been done. These individual's became conscious of the space between stimulus and response and utilized it to make different choices. Certainly in the midst of the chaos that was this experiment, choosing to buck the status quo, in an environment of higher education with roles of educator and educated, where clear lines of who was in the authority and who wasn't, took a certain level of courage and fortitude.

So in your own life, who is the courageous person that will stand between you and the totality of your decisions? The answer, both fortunately and unfortunately for you, is that the only person truly able to facilitate that change is you. In all things, under all circumstances, you are responsible for where you are at today. So let's begin to change the story. Whatever analogy suits you, feel free to use it. Close this chapter and begin a new one. Choose a different fork in the road. Take the path less travelled. Begin a new season. Whatever potentially cliched catchphrase helps you to make a different choice, adopt it, write it down and move forward. More than anything though -

if you are going to to choose in - you must stop making excuses. The truth is there are no do overs and no fresh starts. You are where you are because you've chosen to be here. Please do not discount all of that journey because you aren't happy where you've ended up. Course correct and get back on track, using those potentially painful experiences as reference points and markers of your successes and failures.

The fortunate thing is that because you already know the person responsible intimately, you already know all their deepest darkest secrets and there won't necessarily be any surprises. Conversely, because you already know this person intimately and you already know all the deepest darkest secrets, this translates into you knowing all the limiting beliefs you have currently used to hold you back. If you are wiling to look into them. Looking in the mirror is easily the hardest thing to do. But knowing that no one is to be held accountable for your life but you is incredibly freeing. You now know who the one person you need to know is in order to exercise real, sustainable freedom. Get over the fact that you've known them all along and decide to get to work on building a better tool box.

You see, people rarely make a conscious decision to cause harm. I do not believe that people in general are evil and selfish creatures, although at times we may feel that their actions present them that way. People as individuals simply have an inadequate tool box. Take any tradesman you know and ask to look in their 'kit'. You won't find a plumber lugging around a table saw. Nor will you see a carpenter with a welding torch. Each tradesmen has their specific tools required to complete the trades they have mastered, and often times you'll see they have all they need and just a bit more. For a tradesmen, most men really, any reason to buy a new tool (read that as a new toy) is a good one. Being prepared with the right tools is a sign of professionalism among other things.

Why then are we so prone as humans to continue lugging around these ill equipped, quite frankly often empty, tool boxes in our own lives? What is the most important trade you can be involved in if it isn't building your best self? Shouldn't we all be equally as excited about getting ourselves new tools, or toys, that will help us to build the best version of ourselves? I for one am always looking at the tools available that will make the project of 'me' an easier endeavor. Every successful person I know that has been kind enough to share their story with me personally has shared, in one way or another, that in order for them to move forward they were required to do these three things:

Get clear on what you want.

Find tools that align you with what you want.

Consistently hone those tools.

Failure to make every attempt to do this will guarantee a failed mission. Any endeavor we embark on is a failed endeavor when we fail to plan, and fail to pack, appropriately. I believe there are two conditions that exist that are clouding our ability to see and move forward clearly:

1) Most likely you aren't properly packed and your tool box is ill equipped. On most journeys you have to get in the car and start it to head off. And so that is a deliberate action, or starting point. Your life, the day to day that is made up of the thousands of micro decisions we make, doesn't need a deliberate turn of the key to get going. You are (most likely) going to wake up tomorrow. You'll be hungry so you'll eat. You may use the bathroom first though. Then you'll get dressed, etc etc. You are already on the journey, and if you are here, you are most likely unhappy and looking for answers, or content but wanting more, and most likely you aren't properly packed and your tool box is ill equipped.

2) And number two.....so is almost everyone else's. You don't realize how empty your tool box is because everyone else is operating from a similar place. Add to this that collectively we are overly and improperly concerned about keeping up with the Joneses. If the circle we associate with is conflicted in the same scenario's we are, then it makes sense we would feel normal. We may very well have a low thermometer for success because comparatively we are within an acceptable range. So unless we are put smack up against someone else's well filled toolbox, we rarely make the deliberate time to look at ours. The default has been adequate, up until now it has been enough to get by, and relatively speaking we are within the norm.

if you are here now, reading this book then chances are you are no longer satisfied with getting by. Something, somewhere along the way has caused you to question that paradigm we call the status quo and so here you are now looking to redefine what that means for you. You are currently looking in the mirror, and coming to some new realizations of your own. This may be a crossroads of sorts for you. This crossroads is very likely an opportunity to bring the chapter you are currently in to a close, and an opportunity to continue your journey and begin writing the next one. I would suggest that if anything in the previous three chapters resonated with you that instead of knocking out one formulaic sequel to the story after the other, you shake things up a bit and continue writing your story, but to write it now from this new perspective.

Gabriel Joseph, Inmate No. 18187-081

Gabriel Joseph is a friend of mine and an inmate at a Federal Prison Camp. He was found guilty of a victimless white collar crime of a financial nature. He is open and honest that he did what they say he did, even though there were layers of protection in place to insure the real estate transactions he brokered were legal and above board. At the end of the day those layers failed him. At the time of the transaction he was a happily married man, a father of two with his first boy expected within a few months. By all accounts he was a successful businessman. In his words he was fairly connected, but also not. As an adult male in his mid to late 20's he was just learning who he was. And typical for that time in a man's life he probably put more value on material things and success than he does now. Life is a great teacher that way. In general this was an average American family. Gabriel loved his wife and family, had a ton of friends who they connected with all the time, faithfully attended church, and was involved in his community. And yet here he is today, a convicted felon, at a Federal Prison Camp for the near and foreseeable future.

On the occasions that I have visited Gabe I am amazed at his attitude of gratitude and his true happiness. I asked him how he was able to maintain that perspective and if he felt there others to blame for his current living arrangements. His response is what prompted me to include his story here. He shared with me this: "It's easy to shift blame, especially when the consequences are so harsh. I could have blamed my upbringing, my lack of education or training, the coaches and mentors that taught me strategies that weren't sound, a business partner that encouraged the activity, a loan officer who gave me inaccurate counsel, or corrupt prosecutors who wanted a conviction at all cost and my own attorney that did a pathetic job at my defense. Perhaps I could blame a broken federal justice system that is harsh in punishment and unbending in doling it out. The list goes on and on. But taking responsibility for my own actions that lead to this consequence is ultimately the right course. I chose my actions. I could have made other choices. Looking back, I should have made other choices. Even though I didn't think I was breaking the law in how I structured and executed the transaction - in the end it does not matter. I chose to do it. I chose to structure it the way I did. I chose my partners. I chose to not seek additional training and education. I chose all those things and I am responsible for my choices. I am accountable as well."

He continued to share with me "I get to choose how I react to my situation and who I become while here and when I get out of prison. I still have 100% control over my choices of who I am to become because of this situation. The love for God guides me overall, but more acutely, the love for my wife and children drive me even more. I always look at what I'm experiencing in the present and ask myself: "What am I learning here and who am I becoming as a result? Am I progressing or digressing? Am I becoming better or worse?"

I can either become bitter or better. I choose to become better."

I ask you to consider this when looking in the mirror and reflecting on your own life. Can you sit with the results of your decisions without shifting blame on others and hold yourself accountable as well?

No problem can be solved from the same level of consciousness that created it.

Albert Einstein

So now what? Step One - Show Up. Every Day. Choose In. Heighten your awareness of the world around you. Determine what it is that you want, and how the environment and activities within that environment support, or do not support that purpose, whatever the mission is. Identify the things that are in alignment for you and ramp those up. Identify the things that do not support you or that are not in alignment with your purpose and mission and then choose different. Either eliminate or reduce contact with them. Choose differently than you have been choosing. The thinking that got you here, assuming *here* isn't the end of the road for you, or where you want to be, won't get you to where you are headed. As the opening quote states, "No problem can be solved by the same level of consciousness that created it." So we must elevate our level of consciousness.

If you choose not to, and do not make these choices for yourself, if you do not set your own set of priorities, then others will surely do it for you. This is not living by design, but rather living by default. Some would argue that this isn't living at all. It is simply existing. We all live in a world where we interact with others constantly

- our spouse, our co-workers, our employer, the clerk at the grocery store or the teller at the bank. And each of us has our own agendas, our own needs and wants and desires. If you do not have extreme clarity on your own needs and desires then the needs and wants of those around you can become the dominating force in your life. How many of us have been in a situation where we needed to consider what we wanted and didn't have the answer, or didn't have clarity on the ripples it would create, intended or otherwise? As a result of that confusion we end up in a circumstance where we become resentful or bitter about it. This is where victimhood rears its ugly head. We believe that others are doing things to us. Unfortunately it is us allowing them to because we lack clarity or understanding. If we had clarity and understanding, or awareness, of the course we were on we could recognize how the actions of others and their impact may or may not be in alignment with our goals much faster. This is what we call claiming your power and being in control. Awareness allows for different choices. And luckily for you and me awareness can be developed.

The first of these random choices that comes to my mind is the all important question of 'what's for dinner?' How often has this come up between you and your spouse or friends? Maybe you aren't hungry at that moment, or you haven't given it any thought what so ever? It's possible that nutrition isn't one of the areas of your life that is a high priority. And so you end up having something unappetizing to you in that moment because you just 'went with the flow'. Someone else made that decision for you. And as you reflect back on it you think 'well, that was, meh?' Sound familiar?

Now in terms of life altering decisions perhaps dinner doesn't strike you as one of the most important ones. And I would say that yes, at least not in a singular sense, you are right. I would also suggest that going with the flow can also be a good thing. Sometimes flexibility and compassion will serve you very well, when you are aware of it and being intentional. But let's take that meal, and the potentially thousands of them that are had by default, and then compare that to your current physical state of being. When you look in the mirror what do you see? Perhaps you are overweight. Are you suffering from high blood pressure, or high blood sugar? Do you have any number of ailments that can be tracked back to a root cause that lies within your dietary choices and overall gut health? I'm betting you can. It is estimated that nearly a third of the 300 million people in the US suffer from some type of digestive health problem. So when we think of the decisions we make as light hearted and innocuous, perhaps it is time to re-evaluate that mind set.

Taking this same concept to a larger scale, lets look at instances in our life that are not as light hearted as our meal planning. Let's apply this same line of questioning to your career, or your choice of livelihood or field of study. Was this a truly deliberate decision? One made from your heart centered and intentionally designed life? Or was this another area of your life where the result was driven by others influence over you, or a result of a lack of clarity. Did you fall victim to the all too common 'It's good enough' or 'It will do for now"? This is the crossroads I want so desperately for people to get to. Because it is never too late to recognize a flawed plan and now is always as good a time as any to make a course correction. To make that course correction you must first understand that you may have been making these decisions under the wrong set of criteria. This is where a heightened sense of awareness of your decisions, large and small becomes critical.

Learning the art of *Leaning In* becomes essential at this point. As we evaluate the areas of our life that we are moving from Default into Deliberate there will most likely become a myriad of emotions or feelings that surface. Feelings of anxiety, resentment, fear, confusion, sadness etc. We refer to these thoughts, these feelings or emotions that are not positive in connotation, as resistance. Entire books have been written about resistance. One of my favorites, and a game changer for me is *The War of Art by Steven Pressfield.* The thing about resistance is that there is only one way to overcome it. And that is to go directly through it. Think about resistance for a moment in the physical plane. Weight lifting is a good example. When you lay down on the bench to perform the bench press exercise the bench is stable and grounded, solidly constructed and provides a wide, affirming foundation. As you raise the bar you have to consciously remember not to arch your back as you press forward to maintain proper form. You instinctively want to lean into the weight to move it.

Reflect back on a time your car may have run out of gas, or stalled out for some reason. Not only is it inconvenient and often a stress inducing endeavor, but when you gather some passers by to help you push that vehicle you have to literally plant your feet and lean into the vehicle to get any type of forward motion started. Any attempt to move it otherwise will be unsuccessful. Our mental and emotional resistance is no different. When resistance appears it is physically or emotionally pressing against you. The only way to successfully overcome it is by leaning into it and moving through it. What happens when you release your applied pressure on the weight bar as you move it away from you? It returns with all its weight into your chest. If you aren't careful it will crush you. This is why you need a spotter when weight lifting. Emotional resistance is the same. If you simply try to push it away you will be forced to hold it at a distance until you can no longer do so. And then all that heavy emotion will come crashing back into you.

There is no over it, around it, or under it. You must go through it. The best visual I can think of to describe this reality is wind. Have you ever been walking down the street, or better still, riding a bicycle, against a headwind? You literally have to lean forward, and depending on the speed of the wind you may have to lean in to a great degree, to keep that wind (resistance) from stopping you in your place. If you choose to stand tall, and simply hold your ground you wont get anywhere. And if you lean backward, or retreat from the resistance, you will be pushed backwards. You cannot go around the wind, or under it, or over it. You must meet her head on, with fierce determination to reach your destination. She may slow you down but you can still inch forward. This is exactly the same physics for your mental resistance.

You.
Must.
Lean.
In.

At least, if you wish to move forward. You can choose to allow resistance to stop you, or to push you back. Just know, and dare I say admit, that your decision is in fact a decision. Whether you make it consciously or not is up to you, as again, you get to decide if you want to heighten your awareness or not.

Showing up, raising your awareness and leaning in also requires being present. In order to make deliberate choices that align with our greatest good we need to be present. Again, not a new concept. Volumes of books are available for you to dive into how to be present, how to get present, and how to remain present. I would invite you, if this concept seems foreign or overwhelming to you, to dig into those. At the end of this book you will find a recommended reading guide for you to explore deeper the ideals presented. Being present is discussed again in chapter six. Until then here are a few ways that you can get started on raising your awareness and developing clarity:

Rest.

Proper, restful sleep is vital. When you are tired and exhausted all the time you are not cognitive and able to make clear decisions. Adjusting your schedule and creating time and space for proper sleep will help you to be more alert and capable of making clear decisions. If you believe you can function at your highest point of contribution on less than 8 hours I'd invite you to sleep for 8 hours a night for 30 days and then re-evaluate. It is possible I'm sure as there are exceptions for every rule. Find the sweet spot for you and then stick to it.

Slow Down.

Part of being aware, and being deliberate, is the art of slowing down. And this is an art form. There are so many sources of stimuli that we can choose to respond to that it is often hard to slow down. Releasing the need for immediacy and snap judgements or decisions. Taking 30 seconds, or 5 minutes before making a decision can be a tremendous tool in making clearer decisions. My wife, and honestly my greatest mentor, has said for as long as I can remember 'If you don't know what to do, don't do anything, the answer will come'. It is sage advice. Advice that took me a few years to heed.

Stop Multitasking.

Now, let me be clear - I built a career out of being a master multi-tasker. I prided myself on my ability to process tasks quickly and seemingly do multiple things at once. My clients and colleagues counted on me to be the one who could get more done in the shortest period of time because I could achieve multiple things at once. Here is the thing though — the brain cannot process more than one thing at a time. So you aren't really multitasking. You're processing one thing at a time very quickly, so quickly in fact that it feels like you are processing many things at once. Here's the rub about doing multiple things very fast. Chances are you aren't doing any of them really well. More than likely you are doing them adequately and possibly sometimes better than average. But not great. And for those living by default, just getting by is good enough. For those living by design, it isn't. When I reflected back on this in my own life this is exactly what I discovered. I was all right to pretty good at a lot of stuff, and not great at any of it. And in that process I let more than I would have liked fall between the cracks. We multitask in an effort to be more efficient. And on the surface that sounds great. Realistically though, if we are going back and picking up the pieces of those items that fell through the cracks, how efficient are we really being?

Another word for awareness could be connected. To operate in the present moment you need to be aware of, and connected to, your surroundings. Sure, if you're focused on a movie, or your designated social media time, then go for it. And if you are at dinner with your wife, be at dinner with your wife. When you are at a concert, be at the concert. Listen to the artist, feel the music. If you are busy taking selfies with your partner or recording the show you are more engaged in getting the right shot, or making sure the frame is accurate than enjoying the show. You paid to see them perform. See them perform. This is when you are most connected to the things around you, when you are seeing, feeling, hearing the environment and the people you chose to surround yourself with. This is also when you can recognize whether the environment you've chosen to be in serves you or not. And you can choose here to course correct if necessary.

The last piece, at least the last piece I'll discuss here, in relation to showing up, is Accountability. Your ability to take ownership of your decisions, and there results, is foundational to your ability to move forward in making better choices. We don't have to make better choices when the cause of our suffering is someone else's fault. Because it is someone else's fault. And we often do not care, or even necessarily realize when we are blaming someone else, or who we are blaming. The primary culprits that come to mind are your boss, your spouse, your kids, or like in my case, my parents. Better still, because we aren't clear on who we are blaming we will often default to some abstract idea to blame — the government, the weather, social expectations or even our horoscope. A strange thing happens when you begin to realize that everything is your fault; there is no one else left to blame. Accountability forces us to take on the current state of affairs and see them as our own choosing. It is a concept we live by in my house. So much so that my children, when they are operating from awareness, will answer a question about their misbehavior with a very sheepish 'because I chose to'. They understand that the core reason for whatever mischief they may have gotten into is their own decision making, intentional or not. The sooner you can take responsibility for your station in life, the sooner your awareness of those decisions will heighten. Because when someone asks you why your situation is what it is, or you start to complain about something going wrong in your life, your only excuse becomes your choices. And now that you know this, the next choice for you to determine is how long will you allow a lack of accountability to continue in your life?

We have somehow reached a point in American culture where we no longer take accountability for our actions. It has become normalized to blame others and shift the accountability to another person. How many of you have said something along the lines of 'she made me do (fill in the blank)' or 'he made me feel (fill in the blank)' or 'I would have done/achieved (fill in the blank) if so and so would have (fill in the blank)' Reality is that none of those blanks are anything except for your justification of choosing NOT to do whatever it is you wanted to do or achieve or feel. It is your attempt at discharging pain and discomfort.

A lack of accountability seems to have become this cultural phenomenon. One that I believe has been perpetuated in media and in our leadership for decades. The first instance I can remember of a broad and seemingly total disregard for accountability was in the mid 1980's during the Iran/Contra scandal. As a small child I remember watching the Iran/Contra hearings on television. It was fascinating to me. The real life War Games and secrets that must have been discussed. As the Cold War was coming to a close and cable news was coming into its own this was a big story. At least that was my perception of it at the time. In 1986 America, and as a boy of 12 years old it was everything to me. I suppose there were many other things a 12 year old should have been interested in looking back on it now. But the reason I share this story, is the testimony before Congress of then

President of the United States, Ronald Reagan and Rear Admiral John M. Poindexter. As they were questioned repeatedly about the arms dealings, conversations had with government officials and various other Heads of State, the responses were unbelievable to me: 'I don't recall, Senator.' Over 200 times the phrase 'I don't recall' was uttered in some fashion or another. And no one really seemed to question them beyond that or press as hard as I would have expected. It was just sort of OK that they didn't recall. Now certainly they knew the answers to the questions much more than they led on and these responses were a legal maneuver to keep who knows what from who knows who. It is unfathomable to me now, and was even more so then that people that smart couldn't remember seemingly important details. And Reagan was an actor before he was President. Seems like his memory, or ability to recall, would be pretty solid.

But that didn't matter. This is what I have witnessed numerous times since, and I'm sure it was not the first time that responsibility and blame were shifted and passed on. Unfortunately it has become a very normal and expected thing to do in government. Since this was following the Watergate Investigation and proceeding resignation of Nixon perhaps too much faith had been lost in our government already. The expectation of honest and transparent Leadership had simply been degraded too far. Certainly that seems to be the case today.

We witness police shootings where all evidence points to wrongdoing and yet seemingly no one suffers repercussions. We have politicians who accept bribes and partake in prostitution and it seems they can just resign from their job and have little to no legal consequences for blatantly breaking the law. What messaging are we sending to the people watching this happen when those who we look to for Leadership offer none, and suffer no consequences, nor do we demand any from them? I have witnessed this slow move away from basic accountability as it has been happening for decades and certainly before the Iran/Contra affair. For me, however, I believe this was the origination of when I started to believe that it was acceptable to blame others and to not accept responsibility for my own choices and behavior. This is why I share this with you. Not to begin a political debate or determine which side was right or wrong. That is irrelevant. What is relevant is that if I was interpreting the world around me through that lens I could not have been the only one. And the examples of this have permeated our culture enough in recent years that it is no longer an inconsequential circumstance but endemic. If we are not operating from a place of awareness and understanding then the stimulus we receive is allowed to influence us in unintended ways. I would suggest that a generation of Americans shared my interpretation and that this lack of truth has prevailed for generations after. If we do not choose to shift the tide back to accountability it will continue to influence generations to come.

"I did then what I knew how to do. Now that I know better, I do better." - Maya Angelou

One thing I want to caution against when it comes to the idea of becoming more accountable and accepting the consequences of our choices as truly ours are the feelings of guilt or shame some may feel when reflecting back on past endeavors, be they failures or ill gotten successes. I certainly struggled with this when I started to become aware of the consequences of my choices and how they affected others. I invite you now to remove these thoughts from your mind. Choose to see them as the falsehoods they are and understand that we are only ever able to operate from the tool box we have in that given moment. You cannot go back in time and relive an experience or correct a mistake. There is no eraser at the end of the pencil of life. You certainly can apologize or atone for wrongdoings that you now know could have been handled differently. And know that the offended party will more often than not appreciate the offer of remorse and healing. The offer of a simple apology is enough to heal most wounds. Include yourself in that exercise as you certainly deserve forgiveness and grace. If we knew better we would do better and the fact that you have made it this far in this book means you are looking to learn and grow. Part of that growth is being able to accept the reality of your choices as they are, and were then, and to move forward with this new empowerment, choosing not to wallow in what could have been. Sit in gratitude in knowing that you have improved.

chapter six

BUILD A BETTER TOOLBOX

To the man who only has a hammer, everything he
encounters begins to look like a nail.

Abraham H Maslow

In order to perform the work, we need the right tools. If the work is to generate better, more deliberate and intentional choices, then the tools need to be designed to help perform those tasks. The toolbox of our lives should be just as diverse and complex as our lives themselves. Keep in mind these are abstract tools, not material. A carpenter is expected to carry a hammer, nails, tape measure and cutting tools. An electrician would not be expected to carry a hammer or nails. If you do not have the proper tools you will be lost, wrenching on 2x4's with a pipe wrench or hitting on the pipes under your sink with a framing hammer is ludicrous. The only result can be more frustration and anger along the way. Your tools need to be specific to your tasks, and in this case we are referring to mental training, which requires tools of thought, tools of accountability and tools of determination.

If this is a new concept to you, or your teachers along the way didn't expose you to the tools you needed then you may be sitting on a pretty empty toolbox. When I went out on my own at 17 years old I know that I most certainly was carrying a toolbox that was Empty, with a capital *'E'*. If I am being honest, I'm not even sure I had a toolbox to begin with! A hard lesson was learned after years of living by default and getting smacked in the face with the same cycle of failure. In her book, Healing Your Family History, Rebecca Hintze writes "Any child who doesn't experience a caring, nurturing, and healthy relationship with his or her mother has an increased probability of overall dysfunction including depression, addiction, and suicide. Poor relationships with the father are equally as destructive." Essentially you are being sent into the world without tools to deal with the circumstances you will naturally face as an adult. This was certainly the case for me from the time I left home until I reached my mid 30's and had what Wayne Dyer refers to as a Quantum Moment.

You don't have to come from a broken home though to have darkness. We all have it. My wife's upbringing by all accounts was pretty awesome and storybook. Her parents have been together for 40 plus years, happily. While not without its challenges there was no abuse, no addiction, nothing that would require years of therapy to undo. And yet she too has had to develop tools for her own unique situations bred out of her childhood. There is darkness and sadness in all of us at some time or another. We are all part of the human experiment. Gay Hendricks in his work *The Big Leap* suggests that children are perfect observers and imperfect interpreters and that this may be the root cause of some of our limiting beliefs that dictate our need to develop better tools.

> "It is not your lack of resources, but your lack of resourcefulness that causes you to fail" - Tony Robbins

So let's talk about failure for a minute. There is absolutely nothing wrong with failure. You could easily decide to welcome it. Failure means you are trying, and it means you are *doing* something. Those who don't fail aren't doing anything to fail at. Where failure becomes a problem is when you either aren't recognizing it quickly enough and course correcting, or when you are working to overcome failure with the same thinking that got you into this mess to begin with. We have all heard that insanity is defined as doing the same thing over and over and expecting a different result. If this sounds like you then this is where the realization that you may need some better, or at the very least *different,* tools to work with would be essential.

Failure without adaptation leads to destruction.

Not having the proper tools is nothing to be ashamed of either. Most of us are lacking in this area. And I believe that most, if not all of us, are making the best choices we can, with the information we have, most of the time. The influences and stimuli you have collected over the years to develop your mental acuity and awareness have gotten you this far. And honestly, you're pretty rad. You are a Child of God, after all, and you are uniquely gifted to live the purpose you were designed for.

So where do you get the tools to do the work of making better choices and more fully live in that purpose? Last time I checked The Home Depot didn't carry them. It would be brilliant if they did, wouldn't it? When I settle in on a home improvement or some other creative project, I start by creating the materials list. Then I review my inventory of tools and fasteners needed, and develop a plan. From there I head down to the hardware store and select the materials I am missing and grab the tools I may be lacking. Now I can get to work knowing I have what I need in hand. Should something go amiss or a revision be needed, I simply repeat the process and make another trip to the hardware store. For the more abstract human development project you are embarking on, things are, well, a bit more abstract. The process is nearly the same though. Review your inventory of tools, and develop a plan. As you move along and discover there's a tool you need, you seek it out and learn it. There just isn't necessarily a brick and mortar store to swing by and grab what you need off the shelf. We are too uniquely designed for that type of solution.

Here we are again, presented with another opportunity to choose. You can reinvent the wheel and go back to the introduction of the species, evaluating all the dynamics of the human psyche and develop all the tools necessary to navigate it, or you can trust in those who are living lives that inspire you and explore what they have to say on the matter. Chances are they have done some of that work already. Chances are strong. I prefer to work as effectively and efficiently as possible, and to get to this purpose driven life sooner than later, so it is probably no surprise to any of you that I chose the latter. I would invite you to do the same.

Vinh Giang is a magician, entrepreneur and keynote speaker. He presented an idea that I fell in love with, dissected and have since adopted and slightly expanded upon. Vinh shared a story about his professional and personal progress being tied to the books he has read, and the authors of these books being recruited into his army. You see, the beauty of books, as he describes it, is that you get this lifetime of knowledge and wisdom narrowed down into a consumable volume. And in doing so you are able to escalate your life experiences by adopting some of this knowledge and applying it to your own experiences. Earlier in this book I presented the importance of becoming a Warrior. Now we are building our support Army in this fight. I highly recommend utilizing those who have gone before us to direct us to the information and tools available. If you consider the opportunities you have today to utilize the gifts and learning of others it is an invigorating and mind blowing time to exist. With the advent of mobile devices and resources such as YouTube and podcasts and audiobooks and wireless headphones and speakers and the prolonged commute many of us partake in you are never without an opportunity to be constantly recruiting and training your Warrior mind.

This is be a perfect time to recall the Slight Edge Principle discussed previously as well. A millimeter of change, amplified day after day, changes the course of your life. Whatever your current level of reading, as it relates to human development is concerned, imagine if you took it up .003 percent starting tomorrow. You would double the size of your Army in one year. Chances are you would do much more than that.

This concept doesn't apply only to books either. Consider the films, videos and television shows you watch as well as the events you attend. It is estimated that the average American watches 4 hours of television a day. That would be 28 hours per week. A . 003% adjustment in that viewing schedule would mean that you watched 5 less minutes of television and replaced it with one video dedicated to your human development. One 5 minute YouTube video that helped you to hone your mental toolbox. Do that over the course of a year and your time in front of a screen will be much more impactful. Or you can take one less evening to see a movie out and go to a lecture. Or get to an all day seminar with the top thought leaders in the areas you are working on. It has often been repeated that you are the average of the 5 people that you spend the most time with. Let's amplify that concept and surround ourselves with people that are like minded and driven. Ones that are working diligently to be the best versions of themselves they can be and that are genuinely wanting that for you as well. Not just in spirit but through action.

Let's take this opportunity to explore the preceding thought for just a moment. It is my understanding that Jim Rohn is the one who first stated "You are the average of the 5 people you spend the most time with." Sit with that for just a moment. Who are the people you spend the most time with? Surely they influence you in numerous ways. Include in that analysis the film and television you watch to the music you listen to. And the social media feeds you participate in. These are often the surface things that bring us together in the first place. Common interests that are the beginnings of the relationship. From there have you found yourself thinking similarly, or being influenced by, the attitudes and personalities of those same people? More than likely the answer to that question is yes. So we have to ask ourselves if those people are raising us up or if they are bringing us down. Only you will know the answer to this and only you will be able to choose what to do about it once you determine the truth. I suggest that if they aren't raising you up you decide to find relationships with people who will raise you up. Because anything else is unacceptable. You deserve to be lifted up,

How do we get those new connections, if they are needed, and increase the average of our circle? One habit that I implemented about two years ago is to do an annual schedule. Each December my wife, who is also my business partner, and I sit down to plan the year. We make it a point that within our annual schedule we get to a business or human development seminar at least once per quarter. We happen to work in a field that is heavily driven by personal development though, so the reality is that nearly every event we attend is centered on personal growth as well as professional. At every event I attend I intentionally connect with people who have similar passions for freedom, similar entrepreneurial spirits and a thirst for forward progress and radical accountability. I am recruiting for my Army. Because when you connect in a relational way to others you discover that they too are looking for members of an Army (they may call it a network or a community, but it's the same thing). These are people you can call on in times of doubt, when you find yourself in the valley of despair, to remind you that you are uniquely suited for this journey; to reconnect you to your *'why'*. If we are truly in fact the average of the 5 people we spend our time with, than let's elevate the people we choose to be around, and make sure we are elevating those who choose to be around us.

This is where execution will become your best friend. If we do not choose to execute differently then we will not get different results. It isn't enough o feel differently about our circumstances, we must act differently within them as well. Ultimately there is a theme running throughout the concept of choice, and it is one of accountability. I would like to elevate that concept to the next level though and invite you to adopt a practice of *Radical Accountability*. How do we execute radical accountability? There are a number of ways to do so and most of them will take us back to being of integrity at its core. Here is one example of how to practice radical accountability that I can share with you and one that I would invite you to start putting into practice. It is meant to help shift your mindset into understanding the importance of sitting in truth and authenticity even when it is hard.

Reflect back on a time, I'm sure you've had at least one in the past week or two, that you were asked by someone to do something with them or for them. In how many instances was your response to them "I'm sorry, I can't, I have to (and you can fill in the blank with any number of excuses)." Let's be honest. Every single one of those *'I have to's'* could be, and more than likely should be, changed to an *'I choose to'*. Because the reality is you get to choose to do the thing you 'have to' do instead. Sure you think you have to go to work because you have bills to pay and responsibilities. Or you have to go to Girl Scouts or baseball or the PTA or attend church services on Sundays. Are you trying to tell me you never called in sick to go to a concert, or get a head start on a vacation? Or missed a church service for a football game? You still have bills to pay and responsibilities to tend to, and yet somehow the value of something else preceded your need to make money that particular day. This is called choosing based on priority. I have no judgement about any of those choices. Honesty is a good thing though. So ask yourself how honest are you being when you say "I can't because I have to do…" whatever it is that is actually a higher priority for you than the declined event?

This forces us to then ask, how comfortable are you telling your friend "no, I don't want to come to your kids birthday party because I choose to stay home and do laundry?" or "No, I can't help you move because I had a long week and I'm tired." I believe we don't decline invitations honestly because we don't want to hurt feelings, which is perhaps exercising compassion and maybe even proper etiquette. If you are implementing a designed life, etiquette can take a flying leap. More importantly being proper can sometimes also create a false sense of exaggerated responsibility and it puts you in a space of placing blame (shifting discomfort). It will often also create a space where you find yourself holding resentment for the things you 'have to do'.

By referencing the things we choose to do, regardless of the drivers behind that choice, as things we have to do may seem to you as inconsequential at first. I would argue however that there is an underlying psychological effect at play when we constantly feel like we have to do things, especially things that maybe aren't really exciting. We often view these things as work, or hard, or without much enthusiasm. This is definitely a first world problem. Imagine how different your perspective would be if you lost your job and no longer could go to work. Or if you didn't have the funds to support your kids in their sporting events. Then you would talk about what you wish you could do. Tell yourself you 'have to' take your 6 year old to dance lessons and eventually you'll find yourself not enjoying that time with her. That is an unfortunate and unintended consequence of not embracing radical accountability. Perhaps now is the time to sit in gratitude of the things you currently reference as having to do as things you *get* to do, and *choose* to do. Not with the intention of hurting peoples feelings when you decline an invitation, but as an opportunity to take responsibility for the choices you are making and realizing that you aren't being victimized by the things you have to do. I believe that your new found level of honesty and directness with those you love will be appreciated. It will also empower them to stand in their own power. Yet another ripple you will leave to better those around you.

The difference in radical accountability is that you shed all the blame and resentment you may feel towards others and wholeheartedly accept that you are the only person responsible for your choices and thereby your happiness or lack thereof. Instead of discharging discomfort and blaming others, let's learn to get comfortable being uncomfortable and radically accountable simultaneously. Once we do that, the resulting path forward is simple - stop focusing all your attention on the results of what you have to do, and start measuring your execution of the activities you choose to do.

I believe too many of us are focused on the results, where we are right now, in this time and place without considering what got us here, or the execution. We reference the people we know by their status or what they have achieved - the lawyer, the doctor, the mechanic, the football player, the stay at home mom. With these labels we then categorize who these people are. In addition we look at the result of the activities we pursue as success or failures. Did I sell enough widgets today? Did my facebook post get enough likes or is my latest tweet trending? Did all the right people show up to the party? We are focused on the results without considering the journey and what it took to get there. We cannot control the results. We can only control our own feelings, thoughts and actions. How those come together at the end of the day and what the result of that is, quite frankly, is out of our control. The fact that you took the journey, in my opinion, means you are a success. Regardless of how the results shaped up.

So are you where you want to be? Let's assume for the moment that the answer is no. This is why this book interested you and you've made it this far into it. Consider that there are two primary ways to view this potentially unfortunate result. The first is that you are a victim of the outside world and that despite all of your best efforts you aren't achieving your goals. I would hope that if you felt that way when you started reading this book, that by now you realize that you are not a victim of anything. I would also hope that while you still have goals to achieve, simply moving towards them daily means you are in fact succeeding. The second option is that while you may not be where you currently desire to be, as an end result, you already realize that you are better off today than when you started this journey. You are in fact making forward progress and the reason you are making progress is you. This dichotomy can be summarized by a psychological concept known as the 'locus of control.'

People who develop an internal locus of control believe that they are responsible for their own success. They already know that they are the captains of their fate and the masters of their destiny. They know that life is happening for them and that they are the co-creators of their existence. This does not mean that they haven't received help along the way or that they are arrogant or self centered. Quite the opposite actually. People with an external locus of control tend to believe that external forces are determining their outcomes, life is happening to them and that they are simply at the mercy of their fate. These people will often lean towards struggling and have very low ceilings of achievement. All of us to a varying degree operate from one of these two places, and many of us will operate from both at varying times. It is human nature to project that we are accomplished, and responsible for that accomplishment ourselves in the positive, while being victims or effected by others when the results are in the negative. People are willing participants when taking credit for the things in their life that 'they' accomplished - I received an award, I wrote this best seller (see what I did there?), I threw the winning touchdown. Conversely people are quick to blame the ever allusive 'them' when the result is in the negative - they caused this auto wreck, they raised my taxes, they didn't give me the promotion. See the difference?

The reality is that regardless of your locus of control you have to understand that the only thing you can control are your own actions. Everything else falls to an external force. I consider myself to operate from an internal locus of control - I know that I create, or co-create with God's support, my life. I also know that the only thing that I control in that dynamic is my actions. I have no control over the results of those actions. I will execute reading the book, I have no control over the value of the content. I will execute getting to the class, I have no control over the vitality of the presenter or the importance of its content on my future success when I arrive. I will execute the tasks I believe to be valuable to achieving my goal knowing I have no control over the end result of those actions or how people will respond or how external forces will be applied beyond that. I have written this book, I have given it deep consideration. It has been edited for grammar and content and it has had a few rewrites. I believe it to be the best I have to put forward in this time and place. I have no control over the sales, the reviews or the impact it will have. I do what I think will move me in the direction of my higher good, my purpose, and I trust in the Divinity of the journey as I release any expectations of the result. It is the journey I am most excited about and interested in, so I work to be in it's mindful presence each day.

You can choose to do the same. And you can choose to control how you show up in the face of failure. This is the driving force that you must come to understand when we adopt a lifestyle of Radical Accountability: Thoughts and Emotions + Actions = Results. You control your thoughts, your emotions and your actions. The results are uncontrollable. So your focus should be on the equation and not on the result. Are you executing your necessary actions and are you controlling your thoughts and emotions to drive those actions? Each step along the equation is a choice. The solution, the part that falls after the equals sign, that is the piece that is outside your control. You may influence it by your actions but the finality of the result is outside your determination. Their are too many other factors at play, especially when dealing with other people.

The choices you make in the darkest hour are very likely the ones that will define you. It is vital to your ability to move forward that you choose now to take on the the aspects of Radical Accountability and apply them to the details of your execution in alignment with your highest good. It is the only thing that matters and the only thing you can control. To try and control the external forces at play is a fools errand, leading to confusion, anger and all the negativity that comes with it. To continue to blame external forces for the size and effectiveness of your tools and your ability is dishonest.

chapter seven
THE WORK IS NEVER DONE

We are all apprentices in a craft where no one ever becomes a master.

Ernest Hemingway

The more you learn the more you will need to learn.
Each ring of growth around your tree will lead to new
questions and new challenges. These challenges will
require new tools that will need to be acquired. Think
of it as your own personal continuing education
classes. As an Interior Designer there were always new
products and technologies coming to light that would
need to be explored and understood to fuel creativity
and remain relevant in the field. When I worked in the
Hospitality Industry this was no different. New
entertainment options, food offerings, creative ways to
enhance our guests' dining experience. If you weren't
'on trend' you would see a decline in sales. Your life is
no different. As your life expands in abundance so will
the challenges you face. So once again there will be
new and exciting choices to make, some of which will
involve new learning to navigate them.

This process will continue to unfold and consistently
repeat itself forever if you let it. If we aren't in a state of
growth we are in a state of decay. Just as there are
two mental states one can be in, confusion and
understanding, there are two states of existence within
nature: growth and decay. Nothing in nature is static. A
tree doesn't grow to a particular height and stay there.

It either continues to grow or it begins to decay. Similarly, you are either growing or you are not. Sometimes there is a perceived cycle of growth and decay. The dandelion will close up at night only to bloom again in the morning. Trees will lose their leaves and be in a seemingly perpetual state of rest to the naked eye. Only to blossom bigger and brighter once the Spring returns. We often operate in a very similar fashion. We tackle projects, endeavor to learn and grow for bursts, both short and long, with periods of rest and sometimes periods of perceived decay. Without proper attention however you can move into that slothful and slow decline into real decay. So in order for us to truly continue this growth pattern, as nature intended, we must choose to move beyond our comfort zone as it expands wider and deeper, and we must realize now that the work is never done and commit to constant sustained growth. Our journey here on this plane only ends when we take our last breath.

Brendon Burchard, author of the book *The Motivation Manifesto* and a well sought after high performance coach, is credited as saying "Comfort is the enemy of the high achiever. " This may be true in the context of the world of business. In the context of the broader scope of life, I would argue that comfort is also the enemy of the designed life. Those who truly choose to live by design and not just maintain, or live by default, are constantly living outside their comfort level. The challenge here is that a defaulted life is one that is conditioned within us often without our consciously knowing.

Most of us live within the mindset that a journey has a beginning, a middle, and an end. It is this way with books, film, serial television and mostly within our own lives. Our schooling starts in Preschool or Kindergarten, then there's Middle School, then High School and college. College is primarily considered the end. Some professions require graduate degrees and many adults will move on into Master's Degrees or Doctorates. At whatever level you may complete your 'education' at, when you graduate college people ask you 'now what are you going to do with your life?'. Life has been happening for 20+ years already! And yet, in our minds, graduating from college is 'the end' of our learning and the 'beginning' of grown up life. As my millennial children would say, 'time to start adulting.' That period where we find a partner, get married, start a career, presumably at an entry level job, working our way up the corporate ladder, and have some kids. Then we retire. Another 'end'. This time it is the presumed 'end' of our working and productive life. And then we get to 'begin' retirement. Retirement is that time in our lives, off in the distance, somewhere around 70 or 75 years of age in where we are allowed to enjoy the fruits of our labor. Forget the reality that for about 95% of you there is no such thing as the possibility of retirement. Even though we consciously know this, we still look forward to it because we are conditioned to look forward to the finish line, conditioned to strive toward an ending. We are programmed to follow the path laid out to us in school, reinforced by the media. It is, in fact, a fascinating cycle of beginnings and endings we have been conditioned to live within. It is a lifestyle that I think we should begin to reject.

Life began for you when you entered this plane of existence. From that first breath in your mother's arms, you have been alive. We consider this the beginning, although some would argue that it may not be. Perhaps it began in the womb or before. And in all reality we do not know what happens before you arrive or after your physical being ceases to be. Many people have speculated this, certainly many have educated and very probable ideas. Fair enough. But when your body and mind decays and you can no longer interact with those of us here, we do not know that it 'ends.' Perhaps if we were to view this entire journey through a different lens we may have an even more fantastical experience along the way.

So, if I may, I would like to invite you to review the possibility that it may be impractical, and possibly harmful, to live within this standard paradigm of beginning, middle and end.

Certainly there are seasons to everything. Times when you may be more focused on one endeavor than another or vice versa; times when you are centered on family, welcoming a new soul into the fold, developing a project, starting a business. We will dive into the myth of life/work balance a bit later. In the meantime I would invite you however to look at these longer seasons in your life not as cycles, or chapters, that begin and end, but as pieces of the never ending journey (assuming you believe in an after life and that the journey continues regardless of faith) and integral parts of the whole. Perhaps instead of aligning this paradigm like chapters in a book, we view life as a tapestry. Each narrative woven into the next, and born from the previous one. A piece of the whole that is intertwined with the others. Unravel one string and the others will come with it. If you set fire to one piece you can watch the whole thing go up in flames. Care for all the corners and frayed edges with care and tenderness and the tapestry will last you decades, treat you well and keep you warm. When we operate from this cycle of beginning, middle and end we inevitably are looking almost always at one thing: the finish line. We are focused mostly on the results. I have discovered that in doing so we are missing the very thing that is most important, the present. I hope I am not the first one to point out to you that the present (moment) could very well be called *the present* because it is truly the greatest gift we have been given.

Being present, or in the moment, is often an overlooked and much needed practice. As discussed in chapter four, it is this practice of being present that will elevate your awareness and lead you to more well informed and potentially better micro-decisions. One of my favorite examples of mindfulness is explained by Zen Master and mindfulness teacher Thich Nhat Hanh. In an interview with Oprah Winfrey about his practice of drinking a single cup of tea over the course of an hour, also called the tea meditation, he explains:

> You must be completely awake in the present moment to enjoy the tea. Only in the awareness of the present, can your hands feel the pleasant warmth of the cup. Only in the present, can you savor the aroma, taste the sweetness, appreciate the delicacy. If you are ruminating about the past, or worrying about the future, you will completely miss the experience of enjoying the cup of tea. You will look down at the cup, and the tea will be gone.

> Life is like that.

If you are not fully present, you will look around and it will be gone. You will have missed the feel, the aroma, the delicacy and beauty of life. It will seem to be speeding past you. The past is finished. Learn from it and let it go. The future is not even here yet. Plan for it, but do not waste your time worrying about it. Worrying is worthless. When you stop ruminating about what has already happened, when you stop worrying about what might never happen, then you will be in the present moment. Then you will begin to experience joy in life.

What would our days be like if we operated from this level of mindfulness?!?! Much slower and perhaps less productive by conventional standards I am sure. Perhaps in the Western world you and I choosing to live in this manner just isn't practical. Perhaps. I would suggest adding a bit more of this mindset into our daily routines would be tremendously beneficial. I would invite you to consider that maybe being more present and mindful would allow you space to be even more productive in the things that truly matter. Much of our productivity is busy work.

As I have explored the world of human development for myself and shared my findings with others as I coach them, I have been asked numerous times 'when do I know I'm done' or 'how do I know when I've gotten there'? I am not sure any of us really knows where 'there' is. What I do know is that the work is never done. As we learn more we will grow more and as we grow more there will be more to learn. With each passing goal there is more to achieve, either financially or personally, and I believe that when we shift the mindset off of the finish line, accepting that there is no real finish to our own work, we can begin to focus more on the present. It is the ability to not focus on the end that allows us to be focused on the now. This is what allows us to remain in a state of growth.

At what point would you be willing to openly say that you have learned everything there is to learn? Or that you know everything you need to know. I am certain that I cannot think of such a time for myself. There is always more to learn and to explore. There is an insatiable need for people in this world to be able to serve others. As I believe we are all here to do. So as you develop more awareness, and depth in your knowledge, you will discover new and varied tools that you get to choose to implement into your day to day lives. This will increase your ability to serve others and be more in tune with your purpose. Our capacity to create as human beings is boundless, only restricted by our current skills and our choices. How many times have you heard stories of people doing seemingly unbelievable things, rising up from abject poverty, overcoming immeasurable odds, performing near miraculous feats to achieve greatness? These people did not do so out of dumb luck. These successes were not happenstance. These inspiring achievements come from consistent and measured growth that was determined and never ending. Actions and consequences that were by design. Conversely, we may know someone or may have heard stories of an individual who's glory days were in high school or college. They won the big game, they invented the breakthrough product or technology and then plateaued. This only happens because they chose to rest on their laurels and stopped growing.

There are only two states of existence: Growth or Decay.

Our bodies will eventually follow the course of nature and begin to breakdown. This is inevitable and outside of our control. We will almost always be able to control our thoughts and our choices though. You will get to choose when you plateau or you will get to choose not to. My hope is that whatever path you are on and whatever the journey is for you the choice is to continue to grow every single day.

The surest test of discipline is its absence

Clara Barton

You can not pour into others unless your cup is overflowing. While living a life of your own design will often evolve from finding, then exploring, and finally living in purpose, it is important to understand and accept that your ability to serve humanity at your highest good effectively and sustainably only truly comes after your own cup is full; whatever that means for you. It can show up in numerous ways and circumstances with those circumstances often being as varied and unique as the snowflakes in a blizzard. As discussed in Chapter Six, there are two states in nature: growth and decay. Keeping your cup full will certainly support the growth phase, and can possibly delay that of physical decay if you choose. The solution to how we manifest living with an overflowing cup is within our decision making power.

As we have discussed throughout this book, we all have choices to make, and the choices we make determine our actions, and the consequences of those actions determine the reality of our lives. We have talked about these decisions and how they affect us in primarily abstract terms - meaning it has been so far presented in the context of how those decisions affect our wellbeing; how we feel, our emotional state, and how we are currently existing in this time and place.

How many of us though are living within our physical bodies with that same level of deliberateness? Do you consciously determine what goes into, or on, your body in terms of food, drink, drugs and other consumables? Our physical being is an amazingly complex machine, working in various capacities well beyond what our conscious mind can comprehend. And yet we are primarily responsible for what goes into it. This is relative to both your mental and emotional states as well as your physical one.

There was a time when I did not give the idea of how I was taking care of my physical self a bit of consideration. I would eat whatever I wanted without considering the source, let alone the end result. I would exercise or find movement if the occasion arose, but rarely without deliberate and intended execution. The few times in my life I would end up in a gym were typically centered around the new year, out of the traditional and obligatory 'time to get myself back into shape' mentality. The ironic thing about that is, quite frankly, that we cannot properly tune our mind and utilize it to it's full capacity without first taking care of the rest of our physical being. If we are not getting proper nutrition, rest, and movement of the body to enact the lymph system our bodies become weak or ill. When your body is weak your mind is no longer able to operate at 100% capacity. So why is it that many of us read the books and do the work to meet our thoughts and emotions with understanding, sharpening these abstract tools used to live a heart or mind centered life, without often considering the key thing we need to do to provide a proper foundation for exceptional mental acuity which is optimal physical health as well?

If we are to take the preceding chapters seriously then we must also look at our current state of physical fitness in conjunction with the rest. The primary areas that every one of us needs to be operating from should be rooted in sound nutrition, rest and physical activity. Study after study has been done on successful people and their personal as well as professional habits. In interview after interview greater than 90% of the successful CEO's and entrepreneurs and otherwise financially and socially impactful success stories you will find that they work out regularly. They exercise in some fashion. Whether it is crossfit, circuit training, cycling, running, chi-gong, Krav Maga or simply walking daily with the intention and deliberateness of movement, successful people know that they must move their bodies with intent.

Many people are very aware of this area and are in great shape. The fitness industry is a billion dollar industry with gyms, programs, DVD's, apps, books, trainers, coaches, gurus and all manner of services that you can spend money on from yoga to crossfit to running to cycling to rowing to spinning to boxing and on and on. If this is you, then fantastic. Consider however that these same necessary activities and discipline to maintain a fit and active lifestyle can also become a distraction to prevent you from doing the mental part of the work. I applaud you for loving your physical being and honoring it as it should be, and invite you to sit with the consideration that perhaps some more inward care is needed. It is possible that this is why this book has landed into your life somehow.

Keep in mind also that this concept doesn't need to be reserved for the wealthy or the vain either. There are countless actors, musicians and entrepreneurs who have, as their incomes increased, become more physically fit and nutritionally minded. On the surface this may seem like vanity. I believe that it is something deeper. I believe they had enough of the ingredients for the recipe for success that they were able to achieve success regardless of their physical state. But they soon realized that to maintain it and to have longevity in the game of success that physicality was a larger piece of the puzzle. Successful entrepreneurs and entertainers like Dr. Dre, Gary Vaynerchuk, Jeff Bezos, Drew Carey, Jonah Hill, and John Popper have all transformed physically and publicly shared that it wasn't vanity or ego, but health and vitality that drove them. You are no different than they are.

Your body has to perform various tasks all the time. When it is working harder to perform one task it is not giving attention or energy to the others. So when you are physically struggling your overall machine is having to pull from those other areas, and often it will pull from your mental state of wellbeing which is affecting your ability to make wise choices. Physical movement creates chemical reactions in the body that allow us to function on elevated levels in multiple areas. Brain function, overall immunity, lymphatic and digestive systems, just to name a few, are all positively affected by movement. To deny ourselves of this overall vitality is to deliberately prevent yourself from operating at your highest point of contribution. Low muscle tone, soft bellies, low back problems, lack of mobility, and gasping for breath after a flight of stairs may be some signs that you and the local gym need to get reacquainted. Both physicality and nutrition will impact your ability to maintain overall health.

Additionally, it is no secret that our getting sick, whether it is a short lived acute illness like a 48 hour cold or a chronic issue that may be debilitating, is often the culmination of our choices; food, drink, travel, lack of sleep, and lack of exercise are all conditions that cause our immune system to be working on internal struggles vs seasonal threats constantly. Possibly the most important of these is Gastrointestinal, or GI health, which has been linked to being the root cause of nearly 70% of all major illnesses. We no longer eat well, or supplement properly, and this has lasting effects on our system. Our western society, with its expectations of instant gratification, and fast paced, media overloaded environment keeps us constantly under a barrage of input. Our diets and food choices are often the first to suffer. We are all under environmental threats, at times being exposed to more toxicity and bacteria than I think many of us ever realize. However true that may be, we are living in a tremendous time when supplementation and natural solutions are readily available. It has been a resource for our family that has been a great addition to our health and wellness routine.

There are numerous books and guides to help you determine what is best for you and I am in no way going to attempt to ascertain that for you individually. As mentioned before, in the back of this book there is a Recommended Reading List and there will be some suggestions there for you to explore regarding this topic. What I can suggest is that you examine your current state of nutrition and exercises, identify the gaps in both where there is room for improvement and then *choose to improve*.

The responsibility of maintaining a fit personhood lands on everyone's shoulders. I remember a time in my life when I was achey and slow and I felt like I could not move with agility and ease. Not surprisingly, as we've detailed some of that correlation already, it was a dark time in my life when I took part in drink too often, smoked cigarettes, ate fast food on the daily, and rarely saw the inside of a piece of fruit or a vegetable. Thankfully I appear to be genetically predisposed to rarely getting sick. And that was something I considered a badge of honor. However, when I was to come down with something it would be nearly debilitating. I would be so ill that I would be confined to my bed, seemingly helpless and mentally exhausted. Eventually I realized that I was not a victim of circumstance, I was a product of the result of my choices. Over time I chose to quit drinking, and then to quit smoking and eventually I chose to love the body I was given to carry me through this existence. It has been a process of learning, failing, and starting over. At one time in my life I consumed 6-10 cans of diet soda a day (and no I am not exaggerating for affect), ate mostly meat, potatoes, cheese and fried foods. Thankfully I worked in the service industry and was on my feet most of the time so there was movement, but let's be honest, it wasn't challenging movement by any stretch, nor was it intentional.

So now I make deliberate decisions to get outside, hike, bicycle and move. I watch my dietary nutrition by monitoring what I eat, I supplement well and I drink water, lots of water. I still drink coffee and have dessert when I want. The point is not to imprison yourself, but to choose differently. I simply make better choices more often. And I will continue to love the journey as time goes on. I feel better at 43 than I did at 35, and with 7 kids including a couple of toddlers, that is a good thing. If I am being honest this is the hardest part of my journey and the part that I am still developing tools for. Learning to nurture yourself is hard when you weren't nurtured as a child. I do not share that in an effort to garner your sympathy but in an effort to own the things I need to own and to exercise the radical accountability needed in my own life. To practice what I preach. Recognizing the areas we need work without sadness or grief is vital to developing the tools.

Loving yourself in the physical sense is foundational, and so is loving yourself mentally. To increase your skill in this area and to find the tools you need I would invite you to periodically rank the areas within your life that are meaningful and important to you. Where are you today in terms of nutrition, spirituality, work ethic and exercise? Is it a 5? Or maybe you sit at a 7 or higher. What I would like you to consider is what you need to do to get to the next attainable level? Even if it is moving from a 6 to a 6.5 (keeping the Slight Edge Principle in mind). Once you have determined where you are at within each area, next you can identify 1-3 key actionable items that you can put into practice. One's that will move you from the current number to the next. If your weight is landing at a 6 then perhaps aiming for a perfect 10 in the next 90 days is unrealistic. Instead, let's identify how we can get from a 6 to a 7, or even a 6.5, in the next 30-60 days and diligently move forward in that direction. You are much more likely to be happy with that progress than you are with not reaching the 10.

It is this continual progress, to maintain growth, and not just maintain, that you will naturally perceive as succeeding. You need to see yourself as a success to have a cup that overflows. In order to do this an occasional inventory is necessary to determine where we are at in our journey. This exercise in ranking your current place in various areas of your life, regardless of what ones you may choose, is not meant to send you into a depression. In order to determine how to get where we want to go we must also determine where we currently are. Then, when you are able to objectively see growth and improvement, your brain will have the evidence it needs to support your belief in your progress, your ability and your success. This evidence will assist in creating new neural pathways in the brain that support you mentally in the direction you are headed; and that will help to shift the decision making process you are working to modify.

Throughout my own journey there are some key principles that have been consistent within my learning that have helped me to stay disciplined in this area. I have found that these 5 principles are weaved within almost every philosophy, religion, thought process and lifestyle of successful people. More importantly I have found that people who consistently implement these principles are also decidedly happier.

Enjoy the Journey.

Remember that we are imperfect beings and that the goal is progress not perfection. It is sustained growth over unwanted decay. With that comes the responsibility to stay the course, to Keep. Moving. Forward. Simply loving yourself is an awesome condition in and of itself, and knowing you are in control of the choices you make is going to be foundational in maintaining that self love. Each of us exists for a purpose, and each experience along the way is a reminder of what life is doing for us, not to us, as Tony Robbins says. I invite you to repeatedly sit with gratitude for the gifts that life is putting in front of you. Reflect with joy on your experiences as lessons and experiences that have brought you to today. Tomorrow is never promised. As Marcus Aurelius reminds us in *Meditations,* "You could leave this life right now. Let that determine what you do and say and think." You are the culmination of all these experiences, and they are the result of your choices. Meeting all these fantastic experiences with joy is so much better than the alternative.

Balance is a Myth.

Learn to rest and recharge without expecting equal time for work/family/play. Learn to counterbalance your focus. Work fully now and play some so you can work little and play more later. When you feel like you are losing sight of a particular area in your life shift your focus there temporarily to regain connection and then return your focus on the priority of that season. You will almost never be able to give these things equal focus and energy and attempting to do so will only lead to added frustration. When we set an unrealistic expectation, like balance in this case, we are destined to be disappointed. Remember that anger and confusion are rooted in unmet expectations. Choose to accept the things you cannot control and learn to operate mindfully within the boundaries of them. Balance is a myth that too many of us are searching for. End your search now, prioritize your life depending on the season. Move in and out of those priorities as you need to while living from a place of focus, progress, counterbalance and refocus.

Refrain from Intoxicants.

I don't suggest this from some moral high ground or religious doctrine. This comes from a place of leverage and efficiency. Time is an irretrievable asset. You can make more money, you can grow more food. You can purchase and replace material things. Time however clicks by and cannot be recreated or retrieved. Intoxicants, in any form, alter your mental state and more often than not challenge your ability to make conscious and sound decisions. Quite frankly it opens the door for people to make poor choices. Over time those choices multiply. You do not have a second chance to experience that moment again, to make that choice again. You can always course correct but you can never go back in time (at least not at the current printing of this book). We discussed previously the importance of being present. Intoxicants profoundly impede your ability to do so.

Truthfully, in most cases people do not truly want, nor do they need, to participate in them. People diving into intoxicants such as drugs and alcohol are not going towards a thing they really want, but they are typically moving away from something else, whether it be reality or unwanted emotion and fear. Consider before participating in any of these recreationally what is more empowering to you:

Moving strongly in the direction of your dreams through all obstacles with grace

OR

Using alternative means available to numb yourself from the obstacles along the way?

And, if we are being honest, I believe you do not always need to have Grace. I believe you should be willing to offer it as often as you can, but sometimes you may need to just smash through your challenges however you may, and to do so without the assistance of being intoxicated. Numbing the feelings your journey is bringing to the forefront for you does not proved you the space to adequately deal with them or to understand them.

Consider for a moment the person who wins the lottery. They have everything handed to them quite literally overnight in a windfall of abundance. It is more common than not that they will lose it all in a relatively short fashion because they didn't earn it. They didn't learn how to manage the fear, emotions and the myriad of upper limits that they already possess, or that can potentially come with this level of abundance, so they blow it. For me, this is allegorical to intoxicants. When you choose to partake in these vices you aren't dealing with that which you need to deal with in a clear state, and when the abundance you seek comes to you, the challenges you've numbed yourself to along the way will still exist and most certainly will still need to be addressed. Perhaps even more so now as these issues will be harder to address and harder to resolve when there is much more to lose and they are potentially amplified.

Be Physically Fit.

We opened this chapter on this topic so let this just serve as a reminder. A physically fit person is less likely to fall ill and illness drains your bodies resources; slows you down. It limits your physical capability and creates distractions from the purpose and the designed life you are set upon living. A physically fit person is more likely to be energetic. Energetic people have more vitality, can experience more, and tend to live longer. Experience and vitality are tremendous ways you can expand your tool box. There are 1000 ways to achieve this goal of being fit. Fit doesn't mean perfect or ripped or even thin. It means healthy in body. It means you can do 20 push ups and jog a mile. It means occasionally you will forego the dessert bar for the salad bar. Physical fitness also increases mental acuity. It increases the necessary hormones in your body and it has been shown to aid in decision making and critical thinking. Again, this is an area where volumes of books have been written and this isn't new information. It is however, equally important to your success overall. If this is an area that you rank low in then it is the first I would address. Proper nutrition and supporting of the endocrine system, you know the collection of glands that produce hormones regulating metabolism, growth and development, sexual function, reproduction, sleep, and mood, among other things are more than likely going to do more for the hormonal balance and endorphins you need to operate at 100% than any other tools in your box.

Stay Connected to Source.

Whatever your spiritual path or faith, I personally refer to it often as Source, this is where your purpose came from and where you get your light.

A light needs to be plugged in to be radiant.

When your light is dim, chances are your mental state is one of confusion. Confusion is one way your mind will remind you it is necessary to reconnect to Source. I would contend that all negative emotion should serve as this reminder as well. You can reconnect in a number of ways. Whether it be through daily prayer, meditation, connecting with nature, or reading Scripture, I highly suggest you spend 10-20 minutes every day, preferably twice a day, in this practice. Perhaps use this time in the morning to start your day in peace and gratitude and again in the evening to recharge and wash away the mess that you may have navigated throughout your day.

In addition to implementing these five principles in an effort towards becoming the solution to your challenges and choosing different it is important to talk about a concept that is perhaps over talked about, and yet still important. Throughout this book we have talked about living a life of design and one of purpose.

In modern business terms it seems to be most often referred to as 'Your Why'. I am not sure if this started with the Simon Sinek book, Start With Why, or if his book was written because of this trend. In any event, it is now a part of the American business lexicon and it continues to have relevance. Your Why is very much another term for your purpose. And in talking about you being the solution to your life's challenges, it is vital that you stay connected to this purpose. It is up to no one else to motivate you. Motivation is defined as the reason one has for acting or behaving in a certain manner. It is *your why*. As each of us is uniquely suited for our purpose, it would be unfair for me or anyone else to be expected to provide you with that which is already within you. That comes from Source. It is ultimately up to you to find it, and to stay connected to it. Mentors and coaches you will have throughout life should be expected to inspire you to, and to assist you in, getting reconnected to that why should you ever lose sight of it.

chapter nine

IT ENDS WITH A CHOICE

There are two primary conditions in life: to accept things as they are, or accept responsibility for changing them

Denis Waitley

And so now what? Hopefully as you near the end of this manuscript you have uncovered a few ideas that have brought you value as well as some valuable tools that you can implement along the way as you continue to live a life of deliberate intention; a life of design. In the very least it is my hope that you now know that complaints are futile, because you are exactly where you choose to be. And in coming to this realization you understand that you are now faced with yet another choice: To accept things as they are or to accept the responsibility for changing them.

If you choose to accept things how they are, then you will simply have chosen one of the two paths. Not a good path or a bad path. It is just a path, and since it is the path you chose there is no longer a reason to complain. Nor will you have the right to do so any longer. You will simply know that the things you experience are the result of your letting others choose how they are to be for you; you have chosen to accept them this way. But you will know without any uncertainty that you consciously chose this result. In this case most people will continue to complain though, and they will attract others who like to commiserate in their sadness and despair. Floating along throughout this life forgetting the awesome gift they have been given and the power they hold within to create the life they wish to.

If you choose the latter of the two conditions, to accept the responsibility for creating change, then you are choosing to be a Warrior and to get to work. I won't tell you this is the better of the two choices. If you have made it this far then I don't need to. Who knows, the person apt to decide to accept things as they are, may see the latter of the two options as a futile and frivolous amount of work to be performed by 'those people'. The ideologues and the entrepreneurs who are willing to risk it all and make the rules up as they go along. The rebels and the free thinkers, often called the trouble makers. They may view the way of the Warrior, the internally focused conqueror who lives from a place of lone and radical accountability, as too serious or too driven. And who is to say they are wrong? Who is to say which is better or worse? In the end that type of labeling is all relative. We are not here to place labels on one another or to lay judgement. Just as we do not judge the blind man for not being able to see the sunrise, how can we judge another for not yet seeing their own potential? It is true that when the student is ready the teacher will always appear.

The reality is that what makes each of us truly happy is up to that unique individual. Only that person, in the quiet times, when they can hear their own breath, truly knows if they are content with their choices. By now you should realize that only you have the power to change it if you are not. My only true intention is to help you understand this:

Freedom, and all that comes with it, is yours to choose.

There is nothing else. Nelson Mandela, in his book *A Long Walk to Freedom* said:

> I realized that they could take everything from me except my mind and my heart. They could not take those things. Those things I still had control over. And I decided not to give them away.

All your suffering and pain, your blame, regret and resentment, is self imposed. Mandela knew that with every sunrise, and with every choice presented to him, he had an opportunity to get bitter or to get better. He not only chose to get better, but he chose to use his experience as an opportunity to shift humanity.

Each of us has that capability. Each of us, whether intentional or not, affects those around us in one of three ways - there is always a ripple effect - and it is either positive, negative or neutral (and it is very rarely ever neutral). None of us exists in a vacuum. We all have impact and we are all interconnected. No matter how hard we may try to get off the grid and be self sustaining, we are inextricably interconnected and you will impact those around you. Whether you realize it or not, this is a truth; you do not have to believe or understand for it to be a reality. Reflect for a moment on your day. Where did your breakfast come from? Did you harvest the eggs, or grow the grain, or milk the cow? What about your morning coffee or tea? Let's go even deeper than that. Who built your home? The power grid you use to light it, or the sewer lines that bring you fresh water? All of these things exist in concert with one another at the hands of your community near and far. Much of your existence is predicated on the work of others. The choices they make to show up everyday. For better or worse we all have an impact on those around us. That is a tremendous amount of power.

Assuredly not every one of us will rise to the level of Nikola Tesla, who is responsible for bringing alternating current to the world (you know the stuff that powers everything these days) but you, where you sit, have the ability to shift humanity nonetheless. So I invite you to choose now how you are going to be impactful. Choose now that your impact will be positive and deliberate. It sounds wildly simplistic and yet it truly is fundamentally that simple. In each moment you get to choose: bitter or better, positive or negative. It is irrelevant what the other person is or is not worthy of. That is out of your control. How you respond is your choice to make and your choice to be held accountable to.

With this understanding, when you are now faced with personal suffering in any form, I hope you will take responsibility for changing it, and not simply accept it as it is. I pray that you will be able to recognize the attachment and the unmet expectation that caused it. Because you will be challenged. None of us are able to avoid those things. Just as we cannot avoid thoughts coming to our mind. Even in sleep we dream and thoughts come and go and dance about our heads in ways that we may or may not have ever imagined consciously. We will be faced with things in our day to day that challenge us and require us to go into our personal tool box looking for just the right instrument for the job, assuming you already possess the will to do it. Whatever instrument you choose, however you choose to show up, remember you are in control of that choice. And isn't that the very definition of being free - to live your life under your design?

So Now
What
do
YOU
want?

Resistance

The Art of War, Steven Pressfield

Essentialism, Greg McKeown

The Motivation Manifesto, Brendon Burchard

Confusion

The Four Agreements, Don Miguel Ruiz

Loving What Is, Byron Katie

The Obstacle Is the Way, Ryan Holiday

Acquiring Tools for Success

Leadership and Self Deception, The Arbinger Institute

The Slight Edge, Jeff Olson

Strengths Finder 2.0, Tom Rath (Gallup)

Limiting Beliefs

The Big Leap, Gay Hendricks

Healing Your Family History, Rebecca Hintze

Self Care

The Miracle Morning, Hal Elrod, Pat Petrini with Hanarée Corder

6 Steps to Self Care, Nicole Carter

A Personal Favor

I talk about living by design and taking your cues from those who live the life you want. So I am going to pull a trick from Seth Godin's hat and ask for a personal favor.

First, let me thank you for reading this book and exploring the ideas within. It means the world to me that anyone cares what I have to say and part of my own personal journey has been to practice the art of receiving. I am forever grateful for all the support I have received in writing this piece and your time in reading it. If this book resonated with you and there was anything that you thought to highlight, quote, share or maybe post on your social media feeds, then please give this copy to someone else to enjoy. Or encourage them to snag a copy on their own.

And if nothing here resonated with you then I'd like to ask you to give this copy to someone else who it may resonate with. I appreciate that you gave it a shot at all. While I think it makes a good coaster, it may have more impact in someone else's life as well.

OPERATION UNDERGROUND RAILROAD

My wife and I have been involved with Operation Underground Railroad since May of 2016. It is a cause that we felt immediately called to support. A portion of the proceeds from the sale of this book will be donated to O.U.R. in our continued effort to support their cause. You may recall that throughout this book we discuss that you are the reason you are where you are at, *MOSTLY. The children who are being trafficked are not responsible for their circumstance.* It is up to those of us who have the freedom to help to do so. Please take a moment to visit them at ourrescue.org. The following is from their website:

Since being founded in 2013, we've gathered the world's experts in extraction operations and in anti-child trafficking efforts to bring an end to child slavery. O.U.R.'s Underground Jump Team consists of former CIA, Navy SEALs, and Special Ops operatives that lead coordinated identification and extraction efforts. These operations are always in conjunction with law enforcement throughout the world.

Once victims are rescued, a comprehensive process involving justice for the perpetrators and recovery and rehabilitation for the survivors begins.
It is time for private citizens and organizations to rise up and help. It is our duty as a free and blessed people.

DOMESTIC SERVICES
O.U.R. salutes our nation's law enforcement officers and prosecutors at the federal, state and local levels

who protect our country's children. Law enforcement professionals skillfully investigate, arrest and prosecute those who violate children. Our nation's police efforts to protect children in the U.S. are light years ahead of many, if not all other countries. O.U.R. acknowledges the expertise and extraordinary work done by these dedicated men and women who bravely battle the scourge of child sexual exploitation. O.U.R. shares the mission to save children and seek justice for those who victimize them, therefore O.U.R. is committed to enhancing law enforcement efforts by providing resources where budget shortfalls prohibit a child pornography, child exploitation or human trafficking operation from going forward. O.U.R. will also provide or facilitate child exploitation investigative training in U.S. jurisdictions where a need exists. Collaborating with law enforcement will reduce duplication, promote best practices and avoid other potential issues which might arise without close coordination. O.U.R. is privileged and honored to support our nation's heroes in this important cause to deter, disrupt and dismantle child exploitation and the trafficking of children in our nation's communities.

About the Author

Keith McCoy is a husband, a father and an entrepreneur currently living in Colorado raising his family while growing a wellness business with his wife. Driven by the ideals of freedom, empowerment and radical accountability intermixed with a passion to serve whenever and wherever the need arises, this book is just one of many ways to increase an ever-growing global ripple.

For inquiries or speaking engagements please email choosedifferent@essentialdharma.com

Made in the USA
San Bernardino, CA
04 December 2017